MW00611990

Cinnamon Square

Cinnamon Square

Cinnamon Square

A Measured Approach

Precision Baking with

PAUL BARKER

NEW
HOLLAND

FOREWORD

Having been a keen amateur baker and cake maker for years, my kitchen shelves are stacked with so many recipe books, but nothing like this one. A wonderful idea and strategy to make baking simple and foolproof for all !!!

I've been a regular customer at Cinnamon Square since it opened in 2005 and have always had the most wonderful bread and cakes baked by Paul. Many friends and their children (including my daughter) have had fabulous birthday baking parties in the bakery, enjoying Paul's great teaching style as well as his 'measured approach'.

I think this would be a 'must-have' recipe book to have on hand in the kitchen for all your cakes and breads".

WENDI PETERS
Actress—Coronation Street
Celebrity Masterchef Finalist

"Baking great bread consistently requires skills, precision and passion for the job, day in, day out. It's great to see Paul sharing his knowledge and years of experience throughout the pages of the book. Happy Baking!"

RICHARD BERTINET
Renowned French Chef and Baker
Bertinet Cookery School

Contents

ABOUT CINNAMON SQUARE

The multi-award-winning Cinnamon Square is located on the outskirts of London in leafy Rickmansworth, Hertfordshire. A beautiful Grade II listed building, with low ceilings and with parts dating back 400 years, Cinnamon Square is home to the Bakery Café.

Cinnamon Square first opened in 2005 following two years of meticulous planning and developing the brand concept. A bakery that focused on artisanal baked goods was an essential pre-requisite to its conception. Paul also wanted a place where baking information could be shared with like-minded people and where enthusiasts would be inspired.

Cinnamon Square is a haven for all 'foodies' and its name is synonymous with quality for its exquisite range of patisserie, cakes, artisan breads and handmade chocolates. The breads are made using traditional methods with no additives and the bakery is a member of the Real Bread Campaign—advocating that bread should be made naturally so that it's more nutritional, digestible and that it should remain an important artisanal craft in today's modern society.

Cinnamon Square launched with a signature product—the Cinnamon Square Bun. A sweet, fermented bun, rolled up with a cinnamon filling and topped with a cream cheese frosting. The signature Cinnamon Square Bun was inspired from Paul's travels to the US and Canada, where this type of product is commonplace. Paul made his own version more suitable for UK tastes and the appeal was instantaneous for both adults and children alike.

This product is now part of a range; The Ricky Sticky Bun, the Christmas Bun and the Chocolate Ganache Bun. The range has won four national UK awards including a Great Taste Award and Café Quality Food and Drink Award for the original Cinnamon Bun. Within the first six months of being launched, The Ricky Sticky Bun won a World Bread Award where the judges simply described it as 'awesome'.

The signature Cinnamon Square Bun was inspired from Paul's travels to the US and Canada, where this type of product is commonplace. Paul made his own version more suitable for UK tastes and the appeal was instantaneous for both adults and children alike.

The ethos of Cinnamon Square is based on openness, full disclosure and the use of our senses; where customers can see, taste, smell, hear and touch their whole experience. With this concept came its famous tagline—'The Theatre of Baking'.

Passionate about sharing its baking expertise and knowledge, the team at Cinnamon Square regularly hosts baking masterclasses, children's parties and workshops in 'The Makery'. In fact over 11,000 children were taught over a 10-year period. The sessions are hands on and the children learn about baking in a fun and educational manner, including wearing mini lab coats before entering the scientific baking laboratory. They participate in fun experiments and find out for instance why bread rises and how their senses work.

A truly multi-award-winning and innovative bakery.

PHILOSOPHY AND GUIDE TO PRECISION BAKING

'Measure twice, cut once' is the philosophy of a great carpenter. My baking ethos is that measurement of weight, temperature and time will not only facilitate products of consistent quality, but will also create a more confident and knowledgeable home baker too. There are no cups, spoons or fluid ounces in any of my recipes. Whether I require flour, baking powder, milk or vegetable oil, I weigh them all. And yes, I weigh the eggs too! Therefore I advocate the use of digital weighing scales in grams when adopting my measured approach.

This baking book combines my measured approach with great recipes, many of which are used in my baking school at Cinnamon Square. Wherever possible I have identified each part of the baking process which, if not controlled, will significantly affect the final outcome of your bakes.

For example, there is plenty to consider when kneading bread dough:

- What is the best way to knead bread dough?
- How long do I knead it for?
- How do I know when dough is fully kneaded?
- Can I over, or under-knead?

You will find comprehensive answers to these questions, plus many other important points are explained in a simple manner. The book also provides essential techniques and useful tips, which will enable you to consistently reproduce perfect bakes in your own kitchen—every time.

As a Master Baker of many years, I have the ability to 'feel' my way through the baking process with minimal variation in my finished products. But that comes from decades of experience. A novice home baker will not have this experience to draw from and will have to rely on what is written down in a recipe book. Therefore, any parts of the process, which can be measured or monitored will provide a more controlled 'feel' for the budding home baker. On my baking courses I state that the most important tools for a baker are their hands, closely followed by weighing scales, a thermometer and a timer.

Using these tools, together with the recipes in this book will allow you to adopt my measured approach to your home baking, and ultimately help you to confidently produce fantastic bakes every time.

An important point regarding weighing of ingredients needs to be mentioned here. All the recipes in this book are based on grams (with ounce conversions). Home size recipes can be very small, and by weighing in grams you can achieve precise measurements of each ingredient. However, as you will see, it becomes very difficult to weigh such precise amounts with part ounce equivalents within the recipes. You will discover improved consistency in your baking if you can adapt to using a set of digital scales weighing in grams. Do make sure you choose a set that increase in 1 g or, even better 0.5 g increments. Avoid the scales which increase in 5 g increments, as they are not precise enough. The ultimate home baking scales would be a set that contains two weighing platforms; one for heavy items and the second, a fine set of scales that weighs to an accuracy of 0.1 g—ideal for weighing small ingredients like yeast, salt, baking powder and Cream of Tartar, for example.

Always weigh your ingredients separately too. With the digital scales it is easy to pile them up in the same bowl, but this makes it difficult to remove any accidental excess. Another tip is that for many recipes flour is often the largest quantity ingredient, and therefore will generally be placed in the mixing bowl first, and then the other dry ingredients can be weighed separately and placed on top in separate piles. This is useful to keep check on what you have done—especially if you get interrupted.

Did you know that a cup of flour weighed from the top of a flour bag will be lighter in grams than a cup of flour from the bottom of the flour bag? This is because the flour at the bottom of the bag is more compacted and therefore you will have more grains in the same amount of space. This will cause a significant variation in the consistency of your bakes.

Before making one of my recipes, please read through the instructions a couple of times to familiarise yourself with the ingredients, equipment and any special techniques you will be required to use. A little time spent on planning and preparation with each recipe will reap great rewards.

I hope you enjoy using my recipes in this book and that you also learn a few new techniques too. I truly believe in the potential rewards you will gain from adopting my *Measured Approach* to your baking, and that it will ultimately enable you to confidently make fantastic bakes at home every time.

Best of Baking to you all,
Paul

AN IMPORTANT WORD ABOUT TECHNIQUES

Throughout the recipes in this book we'll be using the same techniques over and over again and there will also be some tips that you'll have to keep in mind in order to get the best results consistently.

In the recipes themselves you'll find the techniques referenced as Technique 1, Technique 2, Tip 1, Tip 2 etc. whichever happen to be applicable at the time for that particular recipe.

Rather than repeat myself endlessly and make the method of the recipe long-winded, I have gathered all the techniques and tips in one easy-to-reference section at the back of the book.

- You'll find the techniques start on page 218.
- And you'll find the tips on page 220.
- There are also a few Facts that you'll need to become familiar with. You'll find those on page 221.
- And there are also some 'How To …' do certain things. You'll find those on page 221.
- I recommend that even before you try the recipes that you read up on the Techniques, Tips, Facts and
- How To's in order to become familiar with what you need to know and do.
- And remember, as important as it is to get the Techniques in your mind conceptually, nothing beats the actual experience of practising with your hands.
- Practise makes perfect.
- Mastering the techniques will take time because real bread takes time and fine baking takes time too.

Large Bloomer £2.20

Breads

Bread is so close to my heart. My first experience of working in a bakery was learning the art of making handmade bread on the night shift. Since this very first experience I have always held a strong passion for bread making. I have since delved deep into the science of bread making and even worked on developing cocktails of additives used in mass-produced bread. Being a true craft baker at heart, my preference has always been to use only the most necessary ingredients coupled with hands on craft skills to make my bread at Cinnamon Square.

REAL BREAD TAKES TIME

Real Bread Takes Time is the ethos. We combine minimal ingredients with craft skills and plenty of time to create breads with better digestibility, texture, flavor and aroma. I express this through the bread we make and the courses that I teach. All the bread recipes in this book are based on my ethos. There are many ways to make real breads—from the quickest method of about three hours to much longer fermented breads which can take days to prepare and produce. I have categorised them in this book under three headings:

- Bulk fermented
- Prefermented
- Sourdough

At my courses I describe the bulk-fermented method as the 'entry level' to bread making and the best method to learn the fundamentals and core skills required to make great bread at home. All these core skills are transferable to the other two methods. Once mastered, you can then move on to the more advanced Prefermented breads. When totally addicted to bread making it is time to try your hand at Sourdough. Each category has a selection of my favorite breads for you to make.

BULK FERMENTATION OVERVIEW

Bulk Fermentation is the most common way of making bread at home and, in general, most recipes found in books or on the Internet will follow this method. If you have and use a bread machine, you will notice it also employs this method. In general, bulk-fermented breads take around 3 hours to make and follow this series of process steps:

- Weighing of ingredients
- Mixing of ingredients to form a rough dough
- Kneading to fully develop the dough
- Bulk fermentation period
- Knock back
- Intermediate proof—resting
- Shaping
- Proving
- Baking

THE BULK FERMENTATION METHOD

When dough is fully developed after a thorough kneading, it is then left for a period of time called bulk fermentation. The duration is generally between 40–60 minutes. Throughout this period the dough matures and naturally continues to produce more gluten and also generates a little flavor. The dough will approximately double in size during this period. After which it is gently degassed—the knock back stage. This 'knock back', breaks down all the large gas bubbles into more uniform smaller bubbles which, when baked, will impart a fine crumb structure to the loaf, typical for English-style or sandwich breads. This also evens out the dough temperature and adds further strength to the dough. The dough is gently rounded into a ball and then given a short period of resting called intermediate proof. This relaxes the dough ready for its shaping. Once shaped, the dough is then proved until approximately doubled in size. This will take about one hour.

Dough temperature, room temperature and the amount of yeast all have an influence on the time the dough will take to prove.

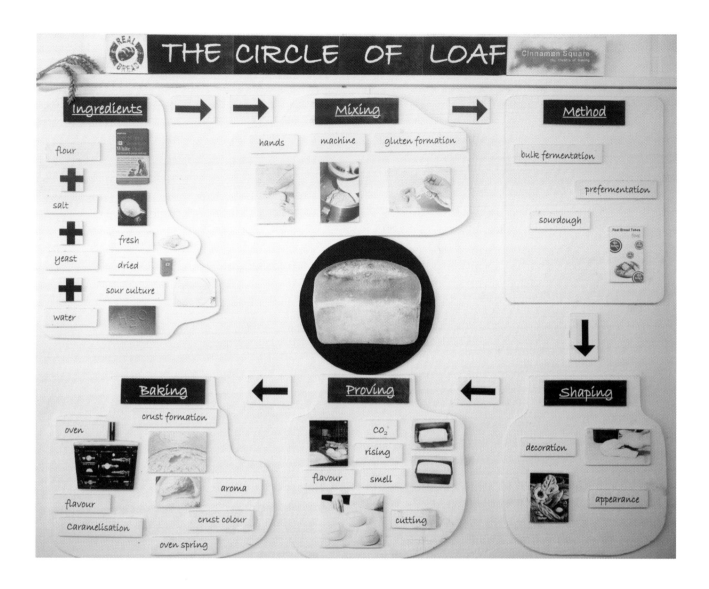

Remember real bread takes time, so don't try to rush this by placing the dough somewhere hot!

To test when the dough is fully proved, you press the dough gently with the tip of your finger. If it springs back firmly then the dough requires further proving. When the dough stays slightly indented then the dough is ready for baking.

Baking is generally carried out at 220–230°C (450–475°F)

PAUL'S TOP TIP

Use an oven thermometer to test whether your oven achieves the correct temperature you have set it to.

English White Split Tin Loaf

This loaf is one I use in my Bread Masterclass as it is an ideal loaf to learn all the fundamentals of making bread. After learning the critical stages of this process, it will put you in good stead for developing your bread-making skills. This recipe produces bread with a lovely crisp top and a moist internal texture, making this the ideal loaf for your everyday use.

Makes: 1 large loaf

Ingredients
600 g (1 lb 5 oz) strong white bread flour
10 g (⅓ oz) salt
12 g (¼ oz) white fat
15 g (½ oz) fresh yeast OR 7 g (¼ oz) dried yeast
350 ml (12 fl oz) water (tepid)

Method
1. Weigh all the dry ingredients separately, then place them in a plastic bowl, flour first then the rest in separate piles on top.
2. Add the water and combine together until a dough starts to form and the sides of the bowl are clean.
3. Remove the dough from the bowl and knead (Technique 1) on your work surface until it becomes smooth and elastic (approximately 12–15 minutes). Use the windowpane test (Technique 3) to check if the dough is fully developed.
4. Form the dough into a ball shape and place in a plastic bowl, cover with plastic wrap (or shower cap) and leave to bulk ferment (Fact 1) for 45 minutes.
5. Remove the fermented dough from the bowl and gently re-round knocking out the large bubbles.
6. Leave smooth side upwards on your table and cover with the plastic bowl for 10 minutes to allow the dough to relax before shaping.
7. Shape the dough to form a sausage/cylinder (Technique 2) the same length as that of the tin to be used.
8. Place the shaped dough, seam side down, into your greased tin (use a little white fat on a paper towel) and leave to prove in a covered plastic box (Tip 1) for 45–60 minutes.
9. When fully proved (Tip 2), spray the top of the risen dough with water and cut surface with a sharp knife (Tip 6) lengthways down the center or in diagonal slashes approximately 5 mm (¼ in) deep.
10. Place the tin in your preheated oven and steam it. (How To 3).
11. Bake at 220°C (425°F) until golden brown (approximately 30 minutes). If the sides of the bread are still white, bake for longer otherwise the loaf will collapse after cooling.
12. Remove the tin from your oven, and then take the baked loaf out of the tin and gently place on a cooling wire rack.

PAUL'S TOP TIP

I recommend using flour that contains wheat that has been milled from Canadian wheat as this will help you make a strong, robust dough that will reduce the chances of making the dreaded 'brick!' The best bread flour to learn the fundamentals of bread making.

Using a scale in grams makes it easy to weigh small amounts

Weigh all ingredients in separate containers including water

Always keep the salt and yeast separate otherwise the yeast will die!

Pour the water on top of the ingredients

Place one hand in with fingers apart and start combining the ingredients

You should end up with a clean bowl before placing on the table

METHOD 1: Knead the dough using the classic method by stretching and turning the dough

METHOD 2: Knead the dough using the Stress Relief method by elongating the dough

Hold on to one end, raise the dough up and...

...slap down on the table, still holding on to the end of the dough

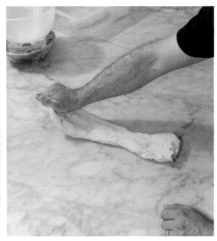

Now roll up the dough but stretch it too

Use the palm of your hand to really stretch that dough

Be really firm with the dough

When the dough is rolled all the way back to a cylinder shape, elongate it and repeat the process

Keep working this dough until it is smooth, elastic and it can be stretched without tearing (windowpane test)

When fully kneaded, round up the dough

Place in a plastic bowl, cover with plastic wrap and leave for 45 minutes.

After 45 minutes bulk fermentation

Remove from bowl

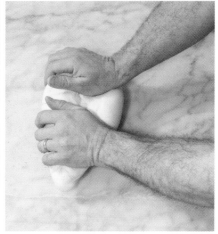

Gently knead the dough to even out the bubble sizes

You can see the large bubbles coming to the surface

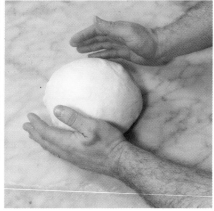

Round up the dough

Leave for 10 minutes intermediate proof before final shaping

After 10 minutes intermediate proof remove to upturned bowl

Turn the dough over so the surface toughing the table faces upwards

SHAPING THE DOUGH: Taking the sides of the dough ball and gently stretch and bang against the table

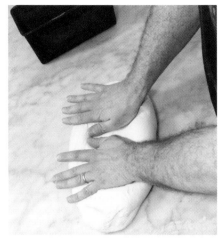

Flatten down into an even thickness

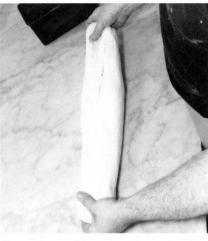

Repeat the stretching and banging against the table procedure

Stop stretching when the dough is about three times longer than the tin

Take the left side of the dough and fold over halfway

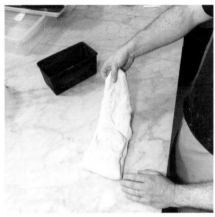

Lift the right hand side of the dough...

... and fold over into a neat square shape

Using the flat of your hands press down to an even thickness

Try to form a rectangle shape (sometimes lifting the dough off the table and placing back down helps to form this shape)

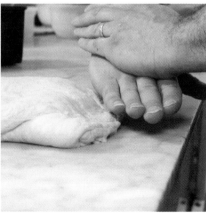

Flatten the edge closest to you to form a tapered edge

Breads

Starting from the end furthest away from you, commence rolling up the dough

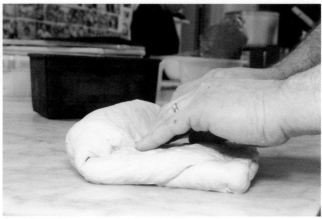

Press down to seal

Continue to roll and seal

The final tapered end to fit neatly as you roll up

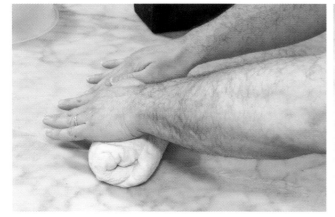

Roll under your hands, like a rolling pin, to even out the thickness along the cylinder (press harder if one end is fatter, but try not to roll longer than the size of your tin)

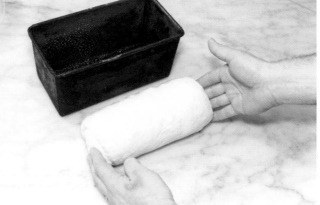

Aim to end up with the dough no longer than the inside of the tin (make sure you have greased the tin)

Lay the dough in the tin with the smooth side facing up and the join (tapered edge) facing down

The dough will expand sideways and upwards to fill the tin

Place the tin inside a tall plastic box with a lid to prove gently for about an hour

Check the dough is fully proved by pressing gently on the top and if it stays slightly indented then the dough is ready for baking.

Spray the top surface lightly with water

Cut down the center of the proved dough. (do not press down with the knife as it will drag and potentially deflate the dough)

This is an ideal depth of cut (approximately 5 mm/¼ in deep)

This shows how the top crust color and appearance change during baking (spraying with water helps the dough to rise evenly and impart a richer crust color).

Breads

Wholemeal Tin Loaf

This loaf requires a little more kneading and attention throughout the process, I normally recommend making this after you have made the White Split Tin loaf a few times at home and you are now comfortable making bread confidently in your own kitchen environment.

Makes: 1 large loaf

Ingredients

600 g (1 lb 5 oz) strong wholemeal bread flour
10 g (¼ oz) salt
12 g (¼ oz) white fat
15 g (½ oz) fresh yeast OR 7 g (¼ oz) dried yeast
390 ml (14 fl oz) water (tepid)

Method

1. Weigh all the dry ingredients separately, then place them in a plastic bowl, flour first then the rest in separate piles on top.
2. Add the water and combine together until a dough starts to form and the sides of the bowl are clean.
3. Remove dough from the bowl and knead (Technique 1) on your work surface until it becomes smooth and elastic (approximately 15–20 minutes). Use the windowpane test (Technique 3) to check if the dough is fully developed. Note that the dough will eventually tear close to the bran particles.
4. Form the dough into a ball shape and place in a plastic bowl, cover with plastic wrap (or shower cap) and leave to bulk ferment (Fact 1) for 45 minutes.
5. Remove the fermented dough from the bowl and gently re-round, knocking out the large bubbles.
6. Leave smooth side upwards on your table and cover with the plastic bowl for 10 minutes to allow the dough to relax before shaping.
7. Shape the dough to form a sausage/cylinder (Technique 2)–the same length as that of the tin to be used.
8. Place seam side down into your greased tin (use a little white fat on a paper towel) and leave to prove in a covered plastic box (Tip 1) for 45–60 minutes.

9. When fully proved (Tip 2) place in your preheated oven and steam it. (How To 3).
10. Bake at 220°C (425°F) until golden brown (approximately 35 minutes). If the sides of the bread are still light in color, bake for longer otherwise the loaf will collapse after cooling.
11. Remove the tin from your oven, and then take the baked loaf out of the tin and gently place on a cooling wire rack.

Points to note when comparing this loaf to one made with white flour:

- Wholemeal breads will take longer to knead to fully develop the gluten and the final dough made will never be strong and robust compared to a white flour dough.
- Wholemeal flour absorbs more water than white flour and therefore the dough made is generally softer and slightly sticky.
- When carrying out the windowpane test (Technique 3) with wholemeal flour dough, expect the gluten membrane to eventually tear close to the bran.
- After the bulk fermentation you will note that the dough should have risen more than a white flour dough would have. It will be slightly stickier and will collapse back quicker when you remove it from the plastic bowl in preparation for the knock back stage.
- Fully-proved wholemeal dough will be very sensitive when ready to be baked, so be very gentle with it when placing in the oven.
- Wholemeal breads are never cut on top before baking as they will collapse before your eyes.

The Oven Bottom Bloomer

This is my longtime favorite bread. When baked, if coated with poppy seeds and baked on the oven bottom for extra crispiness, this makes the perfect all-round bread. The inside should be light and soft and should keep nicely for two—three days.

Makes: 1 large loaf

Method

1. Use the same recipe and method as for the white split tin loaf until you get to the final shaping stage.

2. Shape the dough to form a sausage/cylinder (Technique 2) slightly longer than the split tin, approximately 28 cm (11 ¼ in).

3. Line a baking sheet with baking paper and generously sprinkle with ground rice or semolina.

4. Place the shaped dough seam side down onto the lined tray, and leave to prove in a covered plastic box (Tip 1) for 45–60 minutes.

5. When fully proved (Tip 2), spray the top of the risen dough with water, sprinkle with poppy seeds and cut surface with a sharp knife (Tip 6) diagonally across the surface as many as 13 times (approximately 5 mm/¼ in deep). I find the closer the cut the crispier the crust will be when baked, plus the dough will expand in the oven more evenly and a better looking loaf will be achieved.

6. Place your fully-proved and cut bloomer dough in your preheated oven onto a hot baking stone or upturned baking tray (How To 2) and steam it (How To 3).

7. Bake at 220°C (425°F) until golden brown (approximately 25–30 minutes). If the sides of the bread are still white, bake for longer otherwise the loaf will be soft after cooling.

8. Remove from your oven and place the bloomer on a cooling wire rack.

PAUL'S TOP TIP

I recommend using a serrated tomato paring knife as this cuts fully-proved dough really well with less chance of the dough gripping the knife as you cut or causing collapsing of the dough.

Guinness Loaf

This makes a lovely everyday loaf or a special for St Patrick's Day. Do make sure the beer is at room temperature because the yeast will not be happy in cold beer. You can substitute Guinness for other beers in this recipe, but I would recommend using a dark beer to impart maximum flavor and color to the bread.

Makes: 1 large loaf

Ingredients

600 g (1lb 5 oz) strong white bread flour
10 g (¼ oz) salt
12 g (¼ oz) white fat
15 g (½ oz) fresh yeast OR 7 g (¼ oz) dried yeast
350 ml (12½ fl oz) Guinness (room temperature)

Method

1. Use the same method as for the white split tin loaf until you get to the final shaping stage.
2. Re-round the dough to make a tighter ball shape.
3. Line a baking sheet with baking paper and generously sprinkle with ground rice or semolina.
4. Place the ball-shaped dough, with the nice side facing upwards, onto the lined tray and leave to prove in a covered plastic box (Tip 1) for 45–60 minutes.
5. When fully proved (Tip 2), dust the top with flour through a sieve to give a fine, even coating.
6. Cut the surface with a sharp knife (Tip 6) in the shape of the Guinness logo (approximately 5 mm/¼ in deep). Place the dough in your preheated oven onto a baking stone or upturned baking tray (How To 2) and steam it (How To 3).
7. Bake at 220°C (425°F) until golden brown (approximately 25–30 minutes). If the sides of the bread are still white, bake for longer otherwise the loaf will be soft after cooling.
8. Remove the baked loaf from your oven and place on a cooling wire rack to cool before serving.

Challah Plaited Loaf

I developed this recipe in partnership with one of my customers at Cinnamon Square who was trying to find bread which he remembered eating as a child. This is what we ended up with, a tender loaf with slight sweetness and rich crust color.

Makes: 2 small plaits

Ingredients
600 g (1 lb 5 oz) strong white bread flour
10 g (¼ oz) salt
18 g (½ oz) sugar
18 g (½ oz) fresh yeast OR 9 g (¼ oz) dried yeast
60 g (2 oz) vegetable oil
120 g (4 oz) egg (at room temperature)
192 ml (6½ fl oz) water (tepid)

Method
1. Weigh all the dry ingredients separately, then place them in a plastic bowl, flour first then the rest in separate piles on top.

2. Add the oil, egg and water, and then combine together until a dough starts to form, and the sides of the bowl are clean.

3. Remove the dough from the bowl and knead (Technique 1) on your work surface until it becomes smooth and elastic (approximately 12–15 minutes). Use the windowpane test (Technique 3) to check if the dough is fully developed.

4. Chop the dough into 8 equal parts 125 g (4 oz) pieces. Form the dough pieces into ball shapes and place in a lidded plastic box and leave to bulk ferment (Fact 1) for 45 minutes.

5. Remove from plastic box and gently re-round, knocking out the large bubbles.

6. Place back in the plastic box, smooth side upwards, and leave for 10 minutes to allow the dough to relax before shaping.

7. Elongate four dough pieces to form tapered sausages (fatter in the middle and thinner at the ends 30 cm (12 in) long.

8. Plait the pieces together.

9. Repeat with the remaining four pieces of dough.

10. Place onto a baking tray lined with baking paper and leave to prove in a covered plastic box (Tip 1) for 45–60 minutes.

11. When fully proved (Tip 2), gently paint the dough with beaten egg. Try not to end up with a puddle of egg on the tray as this will burn the bottom of the bread.

12. Place in your preheated oven and bake at 200°C (400°F) until golden brown (approximately 20 minutes). Be very careful baking this loaf as it can burn extremely quickly if the oven is too hot.

PAUL'S TOP TIP

If the loaf does get too dark, lay a sheet of baking paper over the loaf and this will help reduce the amount of further darkening of the loaf whilst still continuing to bake the inside.

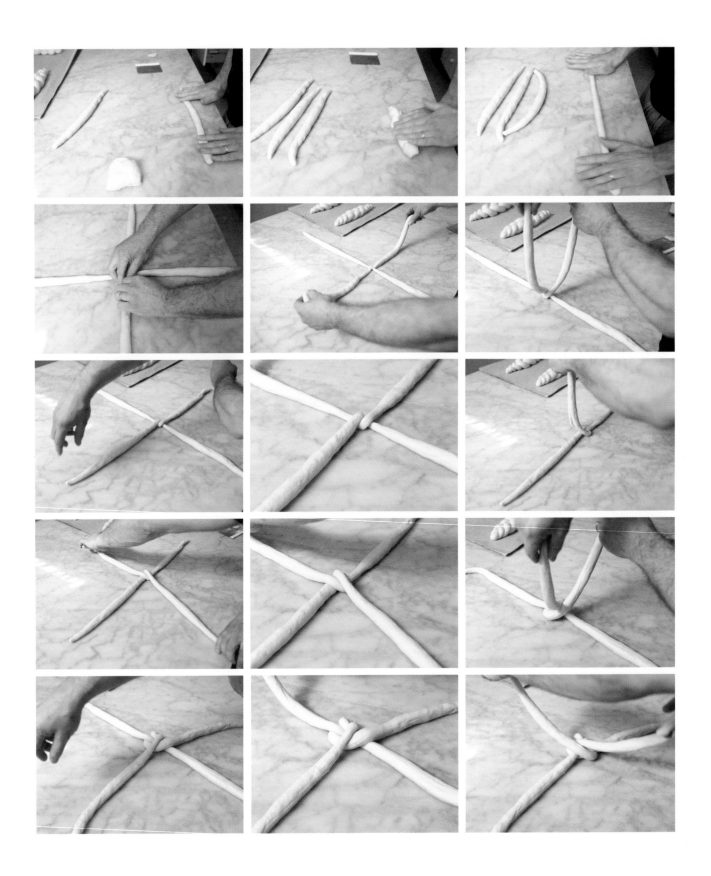

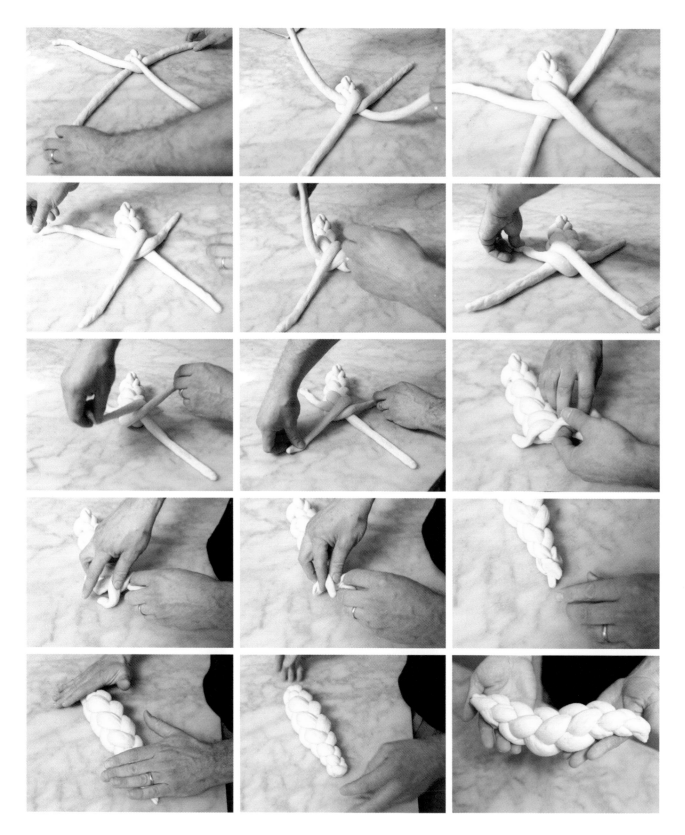

Breads

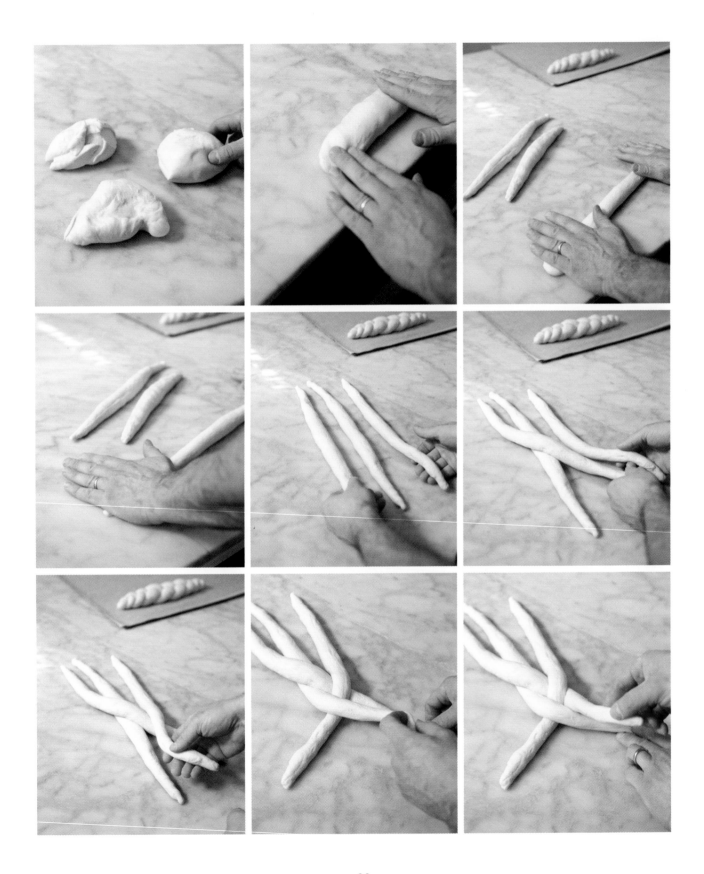

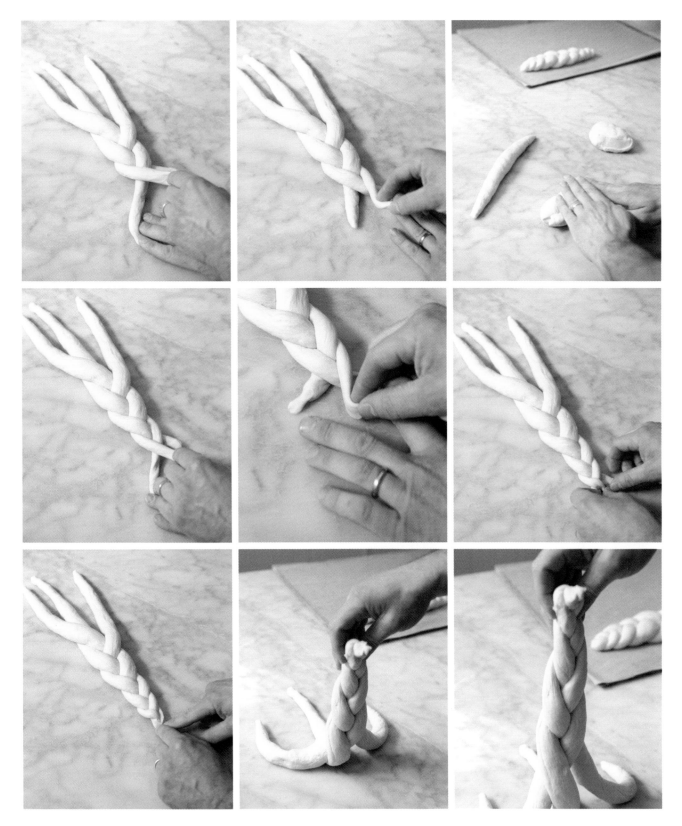

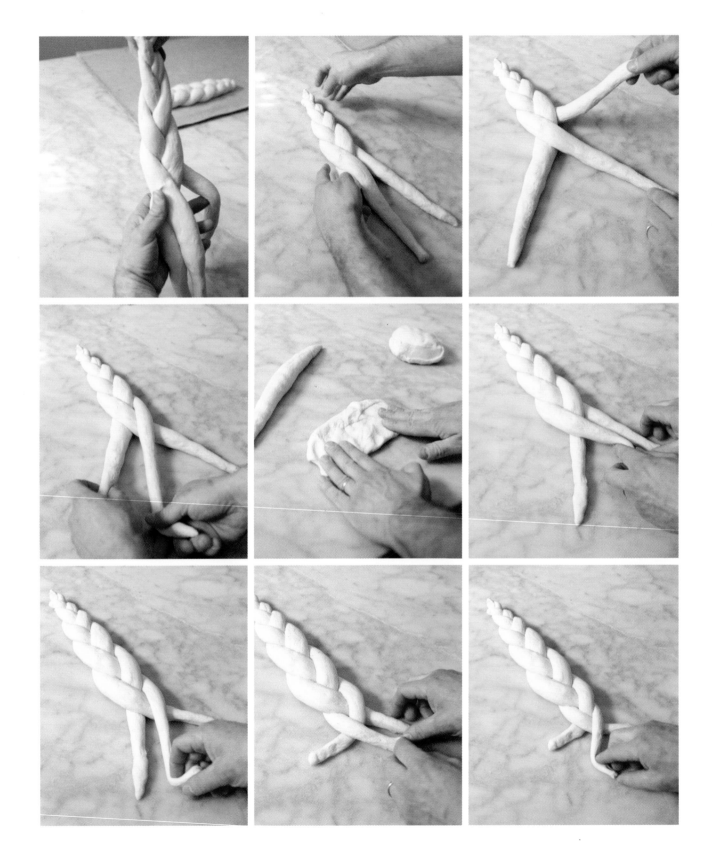

Breads

35

Fig and Fennel Finger Rolls

I developed this recipe for our afternoon tea selection when we appeared on *Britain's Best Bakery*. We presented this with a smoked mackerel filling, so it was loaded with flavor both inside and out!

Makes: 14 finger rolls

Ingredients
450 g (1 lb) strong white bread flour
150 g (5½ oz) wholemeal bread flour
10 g (¼ oz) salt
18 g (½ oz) fennel seeds
15 g (½ oz) fresh yeast OR 7 g (¼ oz) dried yeast
360 ml (12½ fl oz) water (tepid)
250 g (9 oz) dried figs (chopped small)
40 g (1½ oz) walnut pieces

Method
1. Except for the fig and walnuts, make a bulk-fermented dough from the rest of the ingredients by following the instructions to make the Split Tin on page 14. When the dough is fully developed, gently blend through the dried figs and walnuts until thoroughly distributed.
2. Chop out fourteen pieces of dough into 90 g (3 oz) pieces.
3. Form the dough pieces into ball shapes by cupping your hand around the dough and oscillating your hand with pressure against the dough and table.
4. Place in a lidded plastic box and leave to bulk ferment (Fact 1) for 45 minutes.
5. Remove from plastic box and gently re-round knocking out the large bubbles.
6. Place back in the plastic box, smooth side upwards, and leave for 10 minutes to allow the dough to relax before shaping.
7. Elongate dough pieces to form sausages approximately 10 cm (4 in) long.
8. Place onto a baking tray lined with baking paper with the smooth side facing upwards, leaving plenty of space between each piece to expand without touching.
9. Leave to prove in a covered plastic box (Tip 1) for 45–60 minutes.
10. When the finger rolls are fully proved (Tip 2), place the tray in your preheated oven and bake at 220°C (425°F) until golden brown (approximately 15 minutes).
11. Remove from your oven and place on a cooling wire rack.

PAUL'S TOP TIP
* The best way to incorporate the figs and walnuts into the dough is to firstly flatten the dough, then sprinkle the figs and walnuts over the top, roll up the dough and finally, gently knead until evenly distributed.
* You can use this recipe to make two 500 g (1 lb 2 oz) bloomer loaves if you prefer. Follow the instructions as for the Oven Bottom Bloomer on page 25.

Harissa Flatbread

I have seen many ways to make flatbread, some yeasted, some raised with baking powder. It needs to be a yeasted loaf to appear in this bread section of the book, and it is actually my preferred way of making them too. The flatbreads will be baked in a hot, dry frying pan. You can replace the Harissa with your own choice of spice if preferred. I would recommend starting by using the same weight of spice as in my recipe then you can increase or decrease as desired, the next time you make it.

Makes: 12 flatbreads

Ingredients
600 g (1 lb 5 oz) strong white bread flour
10 g (¼ oz) salt
10 g (¼ oz) Harissa spice
12 g (¼ oz) fresh yeast OR 6 g (¼ oz) dried yeast
18 ml (⅔ fl oz) olive oil
320 ml (11½ fl oz) water (tepid)

PAUL'S TOP TIP

You can freeze a batch and take one out at a time when required. Place a layer of baking paper between each flatbread to prevent them from sticking together in the freezer. They can also be reheated to serve warm. If aiming to reheat, do not overbake the flatbread the first time around.

Method
1. Weigh all the dry ingredients separately, and then place them in a plastic bowl, flour first then the rest in separate piles on top.
2. Add the water and oil, then combine together until a dough starts to form and the sides of the bowl are clean.
3. Remove the dough from the bowl and knead (Technique 1) on your work surface until it becomes smooth and elastic (approximately 10–15 minutes). Use the windowpane test (Technique 3) to check if the dough is fully developed.
4. Chop 12 x 80 g (3 oz) pieces of dough.
5. Form the dough pieces into ball shapes and place in a lidded plastic box and leave to bulk ferment (Fact 1) for 30 minutes.
6. Remove one at a time from the plastic box and, using a rolling pin, roll into desired flatbread shapes approximately 18 cm (7 in) diameter. It should not be sticky so try not to use flour when rolling the dough as this flour will burn in the frying pan.
7. Lay the flattened dough into a dry frying pan and bake for a couple of minutes, then turn over to bake the other side. You will have to keep a close eye on this bread to prevent it from burning. You might waste the first few attempts getting the intensity of heat and timings correct but then make a note what works best on your stovetop for the next time you make them.

THE PRE-FERMENT METHOD

The most important factor in making great tasting bread is the long, slow fermentation of the dough. This builds flavor, partly because enzymes break down the starches in the flour into simpler sugars, and partly because as well as carbon dioxide and alcohol, there are other complex flavor compounds which are byproducts of the yeast fermentation process. Bulk fermentation will allow time for the yeast to produce enough carbon dioxide to raise the dough, but not enough time for the enzymes to work or for the development of the other flavor compounds. If we ferment this dough for too long, the gluten becomes too weak to hold the shape of the loaf. So artisan bakers generally use a pre-ferment as a part of their dough. This allows the bread to gain flavor from the longer pre-fermentation and its byproducts, but it will still maintain a strong gluten network for a good rise from the second dough.

Therefore recipes containing pre-ferments will require two doughs; the pre-ferment, which is left for up to 24 hours, and the final dough in which the pre-ferment is added as an ingredient.

Pre-ferments are particularly useful for Italian and French Breads to help strengthen doughs and to increase extensibility respectively. We use them a lot in our breads at Cinnamon Square. Pre-ferments contain commercial yeast (fresh or dried) and are not used to make sourdoughs, which we will cover separately.

Pre-ferments are easy to make and usually consist of a simple mixture of wheat flour, water and yeast (salt is also used in a Pate Fermentée). After mixing, it is allowed to ferment for a period of time, and then is added to a new bread dough within the recipe. On its own it will not make acceptable bread, but when added as an ingredient to a dough it will impart special qualities.

To allow room for the pre-ferment to grow, the ingredients are mixed in a container at least four to five times larger than the mixed ingredients' initial volume. The typical amounts of time allotted for the pre-ferment period might range from 3–24 hours, depending on the dough's temperature and the added amount of commercial yeast. This time might be extended through refrigeration but not for too long and it is best to bring it back to room temperature before use, otherwise it will make the dough it is used in too cold for the yeast to work effectively.

Poolish, Biga and pate fermentée are the three types of pre-ferments.

Poolish is a fairly wet pre-ferment (typically made with equal quantities of flour and water), similar in consistency to that of a batter. No salt is used in this pre-ferment. A Poolish is of Polish origin but used extensively in France and is commonly found in American bread formulations. A Poolish is used to increase a dough's extensibility and is therefore ideal for French baguettes, which require a lot of stretching. A Poolish will also impart more flavor to the baked bread.

Biga have lower water content compared to a Poolish, therefore Biga will feel more like a normal bread dough, only a little firmer. No salt is used in this pre-ferment either. As the name suggests, this pre-ferment is of Italian origin.

As Italian flour will be weaker, the main function of the Biga is to enhance the strength of the dough, but to the detriment of its extensibility somewhat. The Biga also has a positive influence on coaxing more flavor from the dough. Bigas can be held longer at their peak than the wetter sponges like Poolish, which will deteriorate quicker.

pate fermentée is a purpose-made pre-ferment as like a Biga (although can be saved from old bread dough) but it contains salt. This pre-ferment is kneaded to a dough then left for up to 24 hours. This is actually what we use at Cinnamon Square for our English Breads, split tins, farmhouse, bloomers and cottage loaves.

The doughs we make at Cinnamon Square using a pate fermentée generally have a nicer 'feel', with the resultant bread being more flavorsome and richer in color than that of a standard bulk-fermented dough. This is my preferred method of making traditional English breads. We teach this method on our Masterclass in Bread Making course and then compare the results with the more commonly used bulk fermentation method.

Pre-fermented bread recipes will be two-stage processes—the initial making of the pre-ferment and then making of the final dough. In essence, consider a pre-ferment as an ingredient, which you add to your dough to make bread with enhanced flavor and aroma. It normally requires you to make it the day before you intend to make your bread; therefore a little planning is required.

French Baguettes

To make baguettes you will firstly be making a Poolish and leaving it for 8–12 hours. This would enable you to make the Poolish at night and leave to ferment whilst you sleep and then make the baguettes in the morning. The addition of the Poolish will not only impart some fermentation flavor and aroma to the baked bread, it will also help the dough to be more extensible (stretchy) which is important when it comes to elongating the dough to form the classic baguette shape. This loaf should also form a lovely, thick, crunchy crust when baked, making it a 'noisy' loaf to eat. Use strong white bread flour to make this in your first attempt to get used to making the baguette in your environment. After when you have success, try using French baguette flour. The dough will feel softer and you will need to be extremely gentle with it, but you should find the crumb structure inside more open and random when you cut into your baked loaf.

Makes: 3 baguettes

Stage 1—Poolish (prepare 8–12 hours before making bread)
Ingredients
200 g (7 oz) strong white bread flour
1 g (pinch) fresh yeast OR ½ pinch dried yeast
200 ml (7 fl oz) water (tepid)

Method
1. Weigh the dry ingredients separately, then place them in a plastic bowl, flour first then the yeast.
2. Add the water, and then combine together until a smooth, lump-free batter is formed.
3. Leave covered for 8–12 hours at room temperature.
4. It will grow significantly during this period and the top should be covered in bubbles.

Stage 2—Final Dough
Ingredients
400 g (14 oz) strong white bread flour
11 g (½ oz) salt
3 g (⅒ oz) fresh yeast (or 1.5 g (½ oz) dried yeast)
400 g (14 oz) Poolish (made up to 8–12 hours previous from Stage 1)
150 ml (5½ fl oz) water (tepid)

Method
5. Weigh the dry ingredients separately, then place them in a plastic bowl, flour first then the salt and yeast.

6. Add the Poolish and water, combine together until a dough starts to form and the sides of the bowl are clean.
7. Remove the dough from the bowl and knead (Technique 1) on your work surface until it becomes smooth and elastic (approximately 12–15 minutes). Use the windowpane test (Technique 3) to check if the dough is fully developed. This should stretch more than the bulk-fermented Split Tin dough.
8. Form the dough into a ball shape and place in a lidded plastic box and leave for 30 minutes.
9. Remove the fermented dough from the plastic box and very gently stretch the dough and fold into three, then place back into the box and leave for a further 30 minutes.
10. Remove from box and weigh three pieces at 320 g (11½ oz) and gently press them into sausage shapes, without squashing all the bubbles inside the dough.
11. Leave smooth side upwards in your lidded plastic box for 10 minutes to allow the dough to relax before shaping into your baguette.
12. Elongate the dough to the length of your choice, but remember it needs to fit into your oven! I like to dust the top of the baguette in flour as this gives a lovely rustic look to the baked baguette that French bakers make.
13. Line a baking sheet with baking paper and generously sprinkle with ground rice or semolina. You might require two baking sheets to fit your three baguettes on.
14. Place the three dough pieces onto the lined tray or trays and leave to prove in a covered plastic box (Tip 1) for 30–45 minutes.
15. When fully proved (Tip 2), cut the top surface

with a sharp knife (Tip 6) diagonally four or five times (approximately 5 mm/¼ in deep). After the first cut, start the remaining halfway down from the cut previous.

16. Place the dough in your preheated oven, onto a hot baking stone or onto an upturned baking tray (How To 2) and steam it (How To 3).

17. Bake at 220°C (425°F) until golden brown (approximately 20–25 minutes).

18. Remove from your oven and place on a cooling wire rack.

Thin Crust Pizza

The more water you can add in a pizza dough, the lighter and crispier your pizza will be. At Cinnamon Square I use the Ciabatta recipe for my pizza dough. The dough can be rolled out to the thickness of your choice, my preference is thin.

Makes: 4–6 pizzas

Method

1. Use the same recipe as that is used for the Ciabatta in this book.
2. After the dough has been fully kneaded, chop into your desired weights, round them into balls and place them in a lidded plastic box—250 g (9 oz)–325 g (11½ oz).
3. Leave the dough to ferment for 30 minutes.
4. Using a rolling pin and enough flour to prevent the dough from sticking. Roll out to the thickness of your choice—for example 20 cm (8 in)–30 cm (12 in).
5. Pick up and place on a tray lined with baking paper sprinkled with ground rice (to prevent dough from sticking and to add some crunch to the base of the baked pizza).
6. Leave to prove in a lidded plastic box for at least 1 hour (the edges of the pizza should be nice and puffy).

7. Now it is time to get creative with the toppings. Firstly apply a layer of tomato passata, then sprinkle with grated m ozzarella. After this you can add your choice of toppings from olives, roasted peppers (capsicum), cherry tomatoes, meats, chillies etc. I normally finish with a sprinkle of Italian herbs over the top and a drizzle of olive oil before baking.
8. Place your fully-proved and topped pizza dough in your preheated oven or onto a hot baking stone or upturned baking tray (How To 2).
9. Bake at 220°C (425°F) until golden brown, or for approximately 12–15 minutes depending on thickness of dough and amount of toppings applied).
10. When serving, add some rocket to the top to make it look really fresh.

Ciabatta

A very soft dough, which requires a different method of kneading, as it is so sticky. The softer dough allows for the characteristic open and random internal structure and crispy crust to the bread. I would strongly recommend you understand the fundamentals of bread making before you tackle this one! You will be making a Biga preferment the day before.

Makes: 6-8 Ciabatta

Stage 1—Biga (make up to 24 hours before making bread)
Ingredients
162 g (5½ oz) strong white bread flour
1.5 g (pinch) fresh yeast OR 0.7 g (½ pinch) of dried yeast
84 ml (3 fl oz) water (tepid)

Method
1. Weigh the dry ingredients separately, then place them in a plastic bowl, flour first then the yeast.
2. Add the water and then combine together until a dough starts to form and the sides of the bowl are clean.
3. Remove the dough from the bowl and knead (Technique 1) on your work surface until it becomes smooth (approximately 5 minutes). The dough does not require as thorough a kneading as for the final dough.
4. Form the dough piece into a ball shape and place in a lidded plastic box and leave for up to 24 hours at room temperature (around 20°C/68°F–neither too hot, nor too cold) before use as an ingredient within Stage 2.

Stage 2—Final Dough
Ingredients
flour/rice dressing
200 g (7 oz) strong white bread flour
200 g (7 oz) ground rice

Method
1. Stir together with a spoon until thoroughly blended and keep in a jar to be used as a dusting on crusty bread.

Ingredients
600 g (1 lb 5 oz) strong white bread flour
15 g (½ oz) salt
14 g (¼ oz) fresh yeast OR 7 g (¼ oz) of dried yeast
240 g (8½ oz) pate fermentée (preferment 18–24 hours old)
420 ml (15 fl oz) water (tepid)

Method
1. Weigh the dry ingredients separately, then place them in a plastic bowl, flour first then the salt and yeast.
2. Add the pate fermentée and water then, using one hand, bring together until a very wet, sticky dough is just formed.
3. Turn out the wet mixture onto the table and knead until smooth and elastic, using the 'slapping' and 'stretching' action (Technique 4). Keep this going for at least 10 minutes.

4. Use the windowpane test (Technique 3) to check if the dough is fully developed. This should stretch way more than the bulk-fermented split tin dough.
5. At the point when the dough feels smooth and extensible, shape into a cylinder and place into a lidded, olive oil greased (light application to bottom and sides rectangle box approximately 30 cm (12 in) x 18 cm (7 in) and leave for 30 minutes.
6. Remove from plastic box and very gently stretch the dough and fold into three, and then gently flatten to the size of the base of the box. Place the dough back into the box and leave for a further 30 minutes (you could use a rolling pin to gently flatten to give a neater shape.
7. Sprinkle a generous layer of the flour/rice dressing on your work surface large enough for the dough to sit on.
8. Carefully turn the dough out of the plastic box onto the bed of flour/rice.
9. Sprinkle a generous layer of the flour/rice mixture over the top of the dough.
10. Using a metal scraper, cut the dough into rectangles approximately 5 cm (2 in) x 15 cm (6 in). Pressing through the dough sharply to the work surface will cause minimal degassing of the dough (do not use a sawing action).
11. Gently pick up and place each piece onto a tray lined with baking paper sprinkled with ground rice (to prevent dough from sticking). Leave room for the dough to expand without touching.
12. Leave to prove in a lidded plastic box for approximately 30–40 minutes.
13. Place the fully-proved dough in your preheated oven onto a hot baking stone or upturned baking tray (How To 2) and steam it (How To 3).
14. Bake at 220°C (425°F) until golden brown (approximately 15 minutes).
15. Remove from your oven and place on a cooling wire rack.

PAUL'S TOP TIP

When choosing a plastic tub to prove your Ciabatta dough in, make sure the sides are not too high; maximum 100 cm (39½ in). When you tip the dough out onto your work surface it will have less distance to travel, and therefore less chance of damaging the soft, aerated dough as it falls down onto your work surface.

Salt-Free Tuscan Bread

You will firstly need to prepare a Biga up to 24 hours before making this loaf. Only flour, yeast and water are used in this bread. Even though salt is used at such low quantities in bread, it is extremely functional. By removing the salt, not only is the flavor significantly affected but the dough will be softer and stickier, and the yeast activity will not be restricted and therefore the dough will prove quickly. Therefore to make bread without salt we need to adapt the recipe to overcome these negatives. By using a Biga in the recipe we add flavor and strength back and by reducing the water content we make a stiffer, less sticky dough. The shape of the bread you will make with this recipe is rather unusual, but will look stunning when baked. Be prepared for a completely different taste experience with this loaf even though you have incorporated the Biga to impart flavor. It's a bit like being a tea with three sugars drinker suddenly drinking a cup without! Have a few more cups and you get used to it.

Makes: 1 large loaf

Stage 1—Biga (prepare up to 24 hours before making bread)
Ingredients
125 g (4½ oz) strong white bread flour
1.3 g (pinch) fresh yeast OR 0.6 g (½ pinch)
   of dried yeast
60 g (2 oz) water (tepid)

Method
1. Weigh the dry ingredients separately, then place them in a plastic bowl, flour first then the yeast.
2. Add the water and then combine together until a dough starts to form and the sides of the bowl are clean.
3. Remove the dough from the bowl and knead (Technique 1) on your work surface until it becomes smooth (approximately 5 minutes). The dough does not require as thorough a kneading as for the final dough.
4. Form the dough piece into a ball shape, place in a lidded plastic box and leave for up to 24 hours at room temperature (around 20°C/68°F–neither too hot, nor too cold) before use as an ingredient within Stage 2.

Stage 2—Final Dough
Ingredients
600 g (1 lb 5 oz) strong white bread flour
180 g (6 oz) Biga (preferment 18–24 hours old)
12 g (¼ oz) fresh yeast OR 6 g (⅛ oz) of dried yeast
330 g (11½ oz) water (tepid)

Method
5. Weigh the dry ingredients separately, then place them in a plastic bowl, flour first then the yeast.
6. Add the Biga and water then combine together until a dough starts to form and the sides of the bowl are clean.
7. Remove the dough from the bowl and knead (Technique 1) on your work surface until it becomes smooth and elastic (approximately 10–12 minutes). Use the windowpane test (Technique 3) to check if the dough is fully developed. You will note that the dough will take less time to become fully kneaded than a dough containing salt.
8. Form the dough into a ball shape and place in a lidded plastic box and leave for 30 minutes.
9. Remove the fermented dough from the bowl and gently re-round knocking out the large bubbles.
10. Place back in the plastic box for 10 minutes to allow the dough to relax before shaping.
11. Shape the dough to form a tapered sausage (fatter in the middle and thinner at the ends approximately 36 cm (14½ in) long.
12. Place onto a baking tray lined with baking paper and flatten a little.
13. Generously dust the top with flour and ground rice dressing (as used in the Ciabatta on page 44) and then, using a 7.5 cm (3 in) diameter circle cutter (approximate

size) cut three holes right through to the tray (dip the cutter in flour before each insertion).

14. Place into a covered plastic box (Tip 1) and leave to prove for 45–60 minutes.

15. When fully proved (Tip 2), place into your preheated oven and steam it. (How To 3).

16. Bake at 220°C (425°F) until golden brown (approximately 25 minutes).

17. Remove from your oven and place on a cooling wire rack.

Breads

Stilton and Raisin Bread

This recipe is based on my multipurpose base dough. You will need to prepare a pate fermentée first to make this really flavorsome bread. The base dough for this bread is actually really versatile and you can use it to get creative and make other flavor combinations of your choice. In this recipe I have used strong Stilton cheese and raisins. I like strong cheese, but actually do not like to eat Stilton on its own. However, when diluted within a baked loaf it comes across as a more rounded flavor and becomes one of my favorite breads in this book. If you choose to use other ingredients as for green and black olives for example, instead of Stilton and raisins, add them at similar levels to what is used in my recipe. You can always change the levels next time if you prefer. If adding dried herbs like basil, you should weigh a small amount, add them to the dough and then weigh some more if not enough. Record the total weight for next time, when you will only need to weigh it once.

48

Makes: 2 small loaves

Stage 1—Pate Fermentée
(prepare day before making bread)

Ingredients
100 g (3½ oz) strong white bread flour
1.5 g (pinch) salt
1 g (pinch) fresh yeast OR ½ pinch dried yeast
60 ml (2 fl oz) water (tepid)

Method
1. Weigh all the dry ingredients separately, then place them in a plastic bowl, flour first then the rest in separate piles on top.
2. Add the water and then combine together until a dough starts to form and the sides of the bowl are clean.
3. Remove the dough from the bowl and knead (Technique 1) on your work surface until it becomes smooth (approximately 5 minutes). The dough does not require as thorough a kneading as for the final dough.
4. Form the dough into a ball shape and place in a lidded plastic box and leave for up to 24 hours at room temperature (around 20°C/68°F–neither too hot, nor too cold) before use as an ingredient within Stage 2.

Stage 2—Final Dough

Ingredients
300 g (10½ oz) strong white bread flour
5 g (⅛ oz) salt
6 g (⅛ oz) white fat
7.5 g (¼ oz) fresh yeast OR 3.75 g (⅛ oz) dried yeast
125 g (4½ oz) pate fermentée (made up to 24 hours previous from Stage 1)
175 g (6 oz) water (tepid)
60 g (2 oz) raisins (soaked and drained to soften after weighing)
60 g (2 oz) Stilton cheese

Method
5. Weigh all the dry ingredients separately, then place them in a plastic bowl, flour first then the rest in separate piles on top (except for the Stilton cheese and raisins).
6. Add the water and combine together until a dough starts to form and the sides of the bowl are clean.
7. Remove the dough from the bowl and knead (Technique 1) on your work surface until it becomes smooth and elastic (approximately 12–15 minutes). Use the windowpane test (Technique 3) to check if the dough is fully developed.
8. Flatten the dough, sprinkle a layer of raisins over the surface, roll up the dough and gently knead to start evenly distributing the raisins within the dough, trying not to damage the raisins. When nearly completely mixed, add lumps of Stilton cheese and start to blend them into the dough. It is good to have random sized lumps of cheese.
9. Weigh the dough and divide into 2 equal portions, approximately 365 g (13 oz) each.
10. Form the dough pieces into ball shapes and place in a lidded plastic box and leave for 30 minutes.
11. Remove the fermented dough from the box and gently re-round knocking out the large bubbles.
12. Place back in the plastic box for 10 minutes to allow the dough to relax before shaping.
13. Shape the dough to form a tapered sausage (fatter in the middle and thinner at the ends).
14. Place seam side down onto a baking tray lined with baking paper and leave to prove in a covered plastic box (Tip 1) for 45–60 minutes.
15. When fully proved (Tip 2) place in your preheated oven and steam it. (How To 3).
16. Bake at 220°C (425°F) until golden brown (approximately 20 minutes). This bread will obtain a dark crust quickly due to the cheese and you might also find burnt cheese erupting from the dough as it expands and bakes.
17. Remove from your oven and place on a cooling wire rack.

> **PAUL'S TOP TIP**
>
> Instead of soaking the raisins in water, soak them in Port for an extra flavor burst.

Date and Walnut Bread

This recipe is based on my multipurpose base dough but this time we are using dates and walnuts. The baked bread makes a lovely accompaniment to cheese and wine. You could pre-soak the dates in Port for an extra flavor boost.

Makes: 1 large loaf

Stage 1—pate fermentée (prepare day before making bread)
Ingredients
130 g (4½ oz) strong white bread flour
2 g (pinch) salt
1.3 g (pinch) fresh yeast OR ½ pinch dried yeast
80 g (3 oz) water (tepid)

Method
1. Weigh all the dry ingredients separately, then place them in a plastic bowl, flour first then the rest in separate piles on top.
2. Add the water and then combine together until a dough starts to form and the sides of the bowl are clean.
3. Remove the dough from the bowl and knead (Technique 1) on your work surface until it becomes smooth (approximately 5 minutes). The dough does not require as thorough a kneading as for the final dough.
4. Form the dough piece into a ball shape and place in a lidded plastic box and leave for up to 24 hours at room temperature (around 20°C/68°F–neither too hot, nor too cold) before use as an ingredient within Stage 2.

Stage 2—Final Dough
Ingredients
400 g (14 oz) strong white bread flour
6.5 g (¼ oz) salt
8 g (¼ oz) white fat
10 g (⅓ oz) fresh yeast OR 5 g (1/6 oz) dried yeast
170 g (6 oz) pate fermentée (made up to 24 hours previous from Stage 1)
235 g (8½ oz) water (tepid)
80 g (3 oz) dates (chopped and pre-soaked in port (optional)
80 g (3 oz) walnuts (broken into smaller pieces)

Method
5. Weigh all the dry ingredients separately, then place them in a plastic bowl, flour first then the rest in separate piles on top (except for the dates and walnuts).
6. Add the water and combine together until a dough starts to form and the sides of the bowl are clean.
7. Remove the dough from the bowl and knead (Technique 1) on your work surface until it becomes smooth and elastic (approximately 12–15 minutes). Use the windowpane test (Technique 3) to check if the dough is fully developed.
8. Flatten the dough, sprinkle a layer of dates and walnuts over the surface. Roll up the dough and gently knead to start evenly distributing them within the dough, trying not to damage the dates too much as sugar within the dates will come out and cause the bread to bake very dark.
9. Form the dough into a ball shape and place in a lidded plastic box and leave for 30 minutes.
10. Remove the fermented dough from the box and gently re-round knocking out the large bubbles.
11. Place back in the plastic box for 10 minutes to allow the dough to relax before shaping.
12. Re-round the dough again to make a tight ball with a smooth top.
13. Place seam side down onto a baking tray lined with baking paper and leave to prove in a covered plastic box (Tip 1) for 45–60 minutes. Balls of dough generally take a little longer to prove than a sausage/cylindrical shapes.
14. When fully proved (Tip 2) cut a cross into the top surface and then place into your preheated oven and steam it. (How To 3).
15. Bake at 220°C (425°F) until golden brown (approximately 25 minutes). This bread might obtain a dark crust quickly due to the dates.
16. Remove the baked loaf from your oven and place on a cooling wire rack.

Rosemary and Sultana Bread

This recipe is based on my multipurpose base dough but this time we are using dried rosemary and sultanas. This will make a batch of wonderful flavored rolls with bursts of sweetness from the sultanas. I recommend pre-soaking the sultanas in water, then draining them well before adding to the dough, otherwise the sultanas will pull the moistness out of the crumb, quickly drying out the bread.

Makes: 12 rolls

Stage 1—Pate Fermentée (prepare day before making bread)
Ingredients
130 g (4½ oz) strong white bread flour
2 g (pinch) salt
1.3 g (pinch) fresh yeast OR ½ pinch dried yeast
80 ml (3 fl oz) water (tepid)

Method
1. Weigh all the dry ingredients separately, then place them in a plastic bowl, flour first then the rest in separate piles on top.
2. Add the water and then combine together until a dough starts to form and the sides of the bowl are clean.
3. Remove the dough from the bowl and knead (Technique 1) on your work surface until it becomes smooth (approximately 5 minutes). The dough does not require as thorough a kneading as for the final dough.
4. Form the dough piece into a ball shape and place in a lidded plastic box and leave for up to 24 hours at room temperature (around 20°C/68°F–neither too hot, nor too cold) before use as an ingredient within Stage 2.

Stage 2—Final Dough
Ingredients
400 g (14 oz) strong white bread flour
6.5 g (¼ oz) salt
8 g (⅓ oz) white fat
10 g (⅓ oz) fresh yeast OR 5 g (⅙ oz) dried yeast
170 g (6 oz) pate fermentée (made up to 24 hours previous from Stage 1)
235 g (8½ oz) water (tepid)
160 g (6 oz) sultanas (pre-soaked in water and drained)
10 g (⅓ oz) dried rosemary

Method
5. Weigh all the dry ingredients separately, then place them in a plastic bowl, flour first then the rest in separate piles on top (except for the sultanas).
6. Add the water and combine together until a dough starts to form and the sides of the bowl are clean.
7. Remove the dough from the bowl and knead (Technique 1) on your work surface until it becomes smooth and elastic (approximately 12–15 minutes). Use the windowpane test (Technique 3) to check if the dough is fully developed.
8. Flatten the dough, sprinkle sultanas over the surface, roll up the dough and gently knead to start evenly distributing them within the dough, trying not to damage the sultanas too much as sugar within them will come out and cause the bread to bake darker.
9. Chop out 12 x 80 g (3 oz) pieces of dough and form them into a ball shapes and place in a lidded plastic box and leave for 30 minutes.
10. Remove the fermented dough from the box and gently re-round knocking out the large bubbles.
11. Place them back in the plastic box for 10 minutes to allow the dough to relax before shaping.
12. Re-round the dough pieces again to make tight balls with smooth tops.
13. Place smooth side upwards onto a baking tray lined with baking paper.
14. Leave to prove in a covered plastic box (Tip 1) for 45–60 minutes. Balls of dough generally take a little longer to prove than sausage or cylindrical shapes.
15. When fully proved (Tip 2), place the tray into your preheated oven and steam it. (How To 3).
16. Bake at 220°C (425°F) until golden brown (approximately 15 minutes).
17. Remove the tray of rolls from your oven and place on a cooling wire rack.

THE SOURDOUGH METHOD

SOURDOUGH OVERVIEW

Sourdough has been a process for making breads for literally thousands of years. It is a lengthy process but the resultant sourdough breads are more flavorsome, digestible, have lower GI and require no preservatives. Breads made from sourdough are also more nutritious due to the sour elements' neutralizing effect on phytic acid. Phytic acid is found in the bran portion of wheat and it prevents the bran's nutrients from being absorbed by the human body. When making bread by more modern, quicker methods, the phytic acid is still in abundance and renders the bread less nutritious as a consequence.

Sourdough breads are made from flour, salt and water only. Check out the ingredients list on mass-produced bread and you might find up to thirteen ingredients. Maybe not all bad for you, but many totally unnecessary especially when you know that you can make bread using craft skills.

Man's quest for knowledge led to the discovery of yeast and the specific strain (saccharomyces cerevisiae) most suitable for bread fermentation. This yeast is cultivated and concentrated for commercial bread production. For more than a century most bakeries have been using commercial yeast to raise their breads. This helped to increase bread production and create industrialisation of bread by speeding up the baking process—to less than two hours for industrial mass-produced sliced and wrapped bread.

The popularity of commercial yeast led to the demise of sourdough breads and the art in producing it. Fortunately, today we are experiencing a resurgence of sourdough breads due to discerning customers demanding more choice.

At Cinnamon Square we have made sourdough bread since we first opened in 2005. Our philosophy has always been to offer our customers wholesome, nutritious, real bread. We started our own sour cultures in 2005 and have been nurturing them ever since. In 2010 we won a Great Taste Gold Award for our Wheat and Rye Sourdough. We have two sour cultures that we nurture, one wheat-based and the other is made from rye flour. Although they are treated the same you will find that the rye-based sour culture will have a stronger aroma and thicker consistency.

If you have ever researched how to make sourdough breads you might well have been bambo ozled by the complicated recipes and methods found in many books or on the internet. Most over-complicate the entire process and frighten off any novice home bakers. It does not need to be so daunting! Once you have your sour culture established, making bread from it is not that difficult—it just takes time. Keeping the sour culture alive only takes 2 minutes of your time each day. Just think of the sour culture as your home-grown yeast and use it as an ingredient with flour and water to make bread.

So remember, and preach to others our philosophy at Cinnamon Square—'Real Bread Takes Time'.

THE SOUR CULTURE

The first task will be to make your starter culture (your home-grown yeast). This is what you will use to leaven the bread instead of modern-day fresh or dried yeast. This culture is made from just flour and water. It can take around two weeks to achieve enough stability to survive indefinitely, and enough activity to raise bread. Please note, you only have to do this procedure from scratch once. After which, you keep it alive by feeding it daily with just flour and water (when the quantity becomes too big—just throw some of it on the compost and leave yourself a usable amount to continue with).

The culture stays fresh because it becomes naturally very acidic, therefore no moulds or bad bacteria will grow in it. At the same time certain strains of wild yeast (in the air and flour) enter and flourish in the culture. These wild yeasts will leaven sourdough breads. The wild yeasts produce carbon dioxide just like the commercial yeast but at a much slower rate. Therefore we use a lot more sour culture to leaven the bread than we would commercial yeast. In a recipe, when compared to the weight of the flour, we use 1–3 per cent commercial yeast or 40 per cent sour culture (for example, for every 100 g (3½ oz) flour we might use 2 g (pinch) yeast compared to 40 g (1½ oz) sour culture. Even with the vast usage rate difference, the commercial yeasted bread will take only 45–60 minutes to prove before baking compared to 3–6 hours for a sourdough

to reach the same point. This also highlights why the resultant breads are so strongly flavored as so much sour culture is required to provide enough wild yeast to raise the bread.

To make your sour culture from scratch you combine equal quantities of organic flour and water and then feed it daily with half its weight of flour and half its weight of water. Use the table below to keep track on your sour culture feeding regime. Cross off the days as you go. You will note I have used wholemeal flour on day one only. This is optional, but I find it does bring more yeast to the pot which is helpful to get the sour culture active. It is also unnecessary to add other ingredients such as grapes.

SOUR CULTURE FEEDING REGIME

You can use this same feeding regime to make your rye sour culture too. You will find it has a slightly thicker consistency compared to that of a white flour.

Timing	Organic Flour	water (tepid)	Total Weight
Day 1 (the birth of your sour)	50 g (1¾ oz) Wholemeal	50 ml (1¾ fl oz)	100 g (3 ½ oz)
Day 2	50 g (1¾ oz) White	50 ml (1¾ fl oz)	200 g (7 oz)
Day 3	100 g (3 ½ oz) White	100 ml (3 ½ fl oz)	400 g (14 oz)
Day 4 Today it should smell acidic and look bubbly	200 g (7 oz) White	200 ml (7 fl oz)	800 g (1 lb 7 oz)
Day 5 Stir, then discard 700 g into compost and feed the remaining 100 g	50 g (1¾ oz) White	50 ml (1¾ fl oz)	200 g (7 oz)
Day 6	100 g (3 ½ oz) White	100 ml (3 ½ fl oz)	400 g (14 oz)
Day 7	200 g (7 oz) White	200 ml (7 fl oz)	800 g (1 lb 7 oz)
Day 8 Stir, then discard 700 g into compost and feed the remaining 100 g	50 g (1¾ oz) White	50 ml (1¾ fl oz)	200 g (7 oz)
Day 9	100 g (3 ½ oz) White	100 ml (3 ½ fl oz)	400 g (14 oz)
Day 10	200 g (7 oz) White	200 ml (7 fl oz)	800 g (1 lb 7 oz)
Day 11 Stir, then discard 700 g into compost and feed the remaining 100 g	50 g (1¾ oz) White	50 ml (1¾ fl oz)	200 g (7 oz)
Day 12	100 g (3 ½ oz) White	100 ml (3 ½ fl oz)	400 g (14 oz)
Day 13	200 g (7 oz) White	200 ml (7 fl oz)	800 g (1 lb 7 oz)
Day 14 Stir, then discard 700 g (1 lb 5 oz) into compost and feed the remaining 100 g (3 ½ oz)	50 g (1¾ oz) White	50 ml (1¾ fl oz)	200 g (7 oz)
Day 15	100 g (3 ½ oz) White	100 ml (3 ½ fl oz)	400 g (14 oz)
Day 16	200 g White	200 g	800 g

Continue daily feeding and discarding when necessary to keep the total weight to a usable amount.

When the culture smells acidic, looks really bubbly 4–6 hours after feeding and its consistency remains steady, it is then stable and ready for years of baking ahead. You are now ready to make your first sourdough loaf of bread. Do remember to consider this as your home-grown yeast and it is just an ingredient within a bread dough.

Don't be surprised if your sour culture attracts fruit flies–they seem to love it (and chocolate)!

Starting the culture with organic wholemeal flour does make it slightly more active than with white flour. Rye flour will ferment even faster than wholemeal wheat flour and can also be used to start the sour culture process. Revert back to feeding daily with white wheat flour after day one.

If a layer of clear liquid is present on top of your culture–it is probably hungry and you might have missed a feed or two. It should come back to life after a few days of regular feeding. If the liquid is grey in color your sour culture will probably be starving and might not come back, especially if it smells really bad.

You can refrigerate and even freeze your sour culture. When you wish to use it again it might well take a few days or more to get fully active.

PREPARING YOUR SOUR CULTURE TO MAKE SOURDOUGH BREAD

The sour culture requires feeding twice a day for three days before using it to make bread. This allows the culture to become extremely active with wild yeasts. Try to feed the culture at 12 hour intervals and when adding the culture to the dough, it should be at the stage when it is ready for feeding (i.e. 12 hours since its previous feed).

Important note–when starting the daily twice-feeding process, take a fresh container and place only a small portion of your sour culture (i.e. 50 g) in it. Keep the rest of the sour culture in its original container and feed once a day as normal (this is your master stock).

Never continue to daily twice feed the sour culture for more than a few days because it will start to become less acidic.

PLANNING WHEN TO START MAKING YOUR SOURDOUGH BREAD

You need to forward plan as to when you want to bake your sourdough bread. Work backwards to establish when you need to start twice-feeding your sour culture. This is actually a very simple logical process. Let's assume we want to bake some sourdough bread Saturday afternoon. Working backwards, list the process steps and add the timings to each step until we reach day one–when we start the twice feeding process. The table below illustrates this.

This planning example (working backwards highlights the stages required to bake your Sourdough bread, for example on Saturday afternoon.

Task	Duration	Example
Bake	½ hour	Saturday 2.30pm
Final Proof	4+/–hours	Saturday 10.30am
Bulk Fermentation of Dough	2 hours	Saturday 8.30am
Dough Preparation and Mixing	½ hour	Saturday 8am
Day 3 Twice-Feeding	24 hours	Friday 8am and 8pm
Day 2 Twice-Feeding	24 hours	Thursday 8am and 8pm
Day 1 Twice-Feeding	24 hours	Wednesday 8am and 8pm

The entire process in the planning example takes 78.5 hours. The resulting bread should be well worth the wait!

Note–the dough can be made at night and then refrigerated until the morning when it can be removed and allowed to warm up and gently proved. This offers some flexibility on your timings. The resulting bread will have a richer crust color and an abundance of tiny bubbles in the crust called 'fish eyes'. This is due to the longer time amassed between dough formation and baking.

You might well have seen sourdough breads in cane proving baskets. These are used for the softer doughs containing a higher water content. The baskets stop the dough from flowing during the long proving stage. The dough is turned out and placed quickly into the oven and will expand significantly during baking, producing an open and moist texture to the inside of the bread. Sourdough can also be made in bread tins to make a more practical loaf for everyday use. Sourdough can also be made into a tighter dough, which can then be proved and baked on a baking tray. This sourdough will have less expansion during baking and have a denser inside texture to the baked bread.

In summary, once your sour culture is established, keep it fed daily and this will be your master stock that will last indefinitely. You will take some of this sour culture from your master stock to use to make your sourdough bread (you will feed this twice a day for three days to get it really active). Think of the sour culture as just an ingredient within a recipe that will raise the dough, albeit very slowly.

Do not continue to keep the sour culture fed twice daily for more than three days as it will lose its high acidity and, as a result, become less stable; becoming more susceptible to spoil. When I continued to keep feeding my sour twice a day, I noticed a lack of aroma and a change in appearance. I therefore stopped feeding it for a couple of days to let it turn more sour, and then recommenced feeding once a day.

Wheat and Rye Sourdough

This is longtime favorite bread of mine. This bread is so nice it won a Great Taste Gold Award. You will need to have an active rye sour culture prepared to make this bread. This is also a two-stage process as you will make a Rye Biga the day before, which will be used as an ingredient in the dough the following day. However this Biga is made with rye sour culture rather than fresh yeast as for Ciabatta. The final dough will have a firm consistency, and therefore will be proved on a baking tray rather than a cane proving basket; as it will not flow during the long proving stage.

Makes: 1 large loaf

Stage 1–Rye Biga (prepare the day before making bread)

Ingredients
130 g (4½ oz) rye flour
46 g (1½ oz) rye sour culture, twice fed for three days
72 ml (2½ fl oz) water (tepid)

Method
1. Add all the ingredients into a plastic bowl and, using a wooden spoon, stir until a thick, smooth paste is formed. Cover the bowl with a shower cap or plastic wrap and leave at room temperature.

Stage 2—Final Dough

Ingredients
445 g (16 oz) strong white bread flour
12 g (¼ oz) salt
248 g (9 oz) rye biga (all of the above recipe)
250 ml (9 fl oz) water (tepid)

Method
2. Weigh the dry ingredients separately, then place them in a plastic bowl—flour first then the salt.
3. Add the Rye Biga and water, then combine together until a dough starts to form and the sides of the bowl are clean.
4. Remove the dough from the bowl and knead (Technique 1) on your work surface until it becomes smooth and elastic (approximately 10–12 minutes). Use the windowpane test (Technique 3) to check if the dough is fully developed. You will note that the dough will take less time to become fully kneaded than a conventional yeasted dough.
5. Form the dough into a ball shape and place in a lidded plastic box and leave for 60 minutes.
6. Remove the dough from the plastic box and gently stretch it and fold into three, press down, stretch and fold again into three, at right angles to the way you first folded it.
7. Place back into the box and leave for a further 60 minutes.
8. Remove the dough from box and gently form into a ball.
9. Place back in the plastic box, smooth side upwards for 15 minutes to allow the dough to relax.
10. Gently re-round the ball and place smooth side upwards onto a baking tray lined with baking paper, generously sprinkled with ground rice or semolina.
11. Place the tray into a covered plastic box (Tip 1) and leave to prove. This could take between 2–4 hours depending on the activity of your sour culture, but it's normally quicker than for the wheat sourdough.
12. When fully proved (Tip 2) generously sprinkle some ground rice/semolina on your pizza peel or flat thin baking tray, then gently place the dough onto whichever used.
13. Cut a cross or diamond pattern on the top surface of the dough with a sharp knife (Tip 6).
14. Slide the dough onto your baking stone or heavy baking tray in your preheated oven and steam it (How To 3).
15. Bake at 220°C (425°F) until a dark rich golden brown crust is formed (approximately 35–40 minutes).
16. Remove the baked loaf from your oven and place on a cooling wire rack.

San Francisco Style Soup Bowls

It took me fifty years to get there but I finally managed to try an authentic San Francisco Soup Bowl. Lactobacillus Sanfranciscensis is a species of lactic acid bacteria that helps give this sourdough bread its characteristic taste. It is unique to the bay area of San Francisco. Although we can't reproduce the sour culture exactly (unless you live in San Francisco) we can still make our own version of this classic soup bowl, synonymous with being filled with clam chowder. When baked, you cut out a hole in the top crust and pull out most of the inside of the roll. Fill with chowder and serve. When you finish the soup, you eat the bowl!

Makes: 3 soup bowls

Ingredients
400 g (14 oz) strong white bread flour
12 g (¼ oz) salt
240 g (8½ oz) wheat sour culture, twice fed for three days
300 ml (10½ fl oz) water (tepid)

Method
1. Weigh the dry ingredients separately, then place them in a plastic bowl, flour first, then the salt.
2. Add the wheat sour culture and water then combine together until dough starts to form and the sides of the bowl are clean.
3. Remove the dough from the bowl and knead (Technique 1) on your work surface until it becomes smooth and elastic (approximately 10–12 minutes). Use the windowpane test (Technique 3) to check if the dough is fully developed. You will note that the dough will take less time to become fully kneaded than a conventional yeasted dough.
4. Weigh the dough into 3 x 315 g (11 oz) ball shapes and place in a lidded plastic box and leave for 40 minutes.
5. Remove the balls of dough from plastic box and re-round.
6. Place back into the box and leave for a further 40 minutes.
7. Remove them again from box and re-round into balls.
8. Place back in the plastic box for 15 minutes to allow the dough to relax.
9. Gently re-round the balls and place onto a baking

paper lined baking tray. Leave enough room around them so that the balls can expand as they prove and whilst they bake on the tray.
10. Place into a covered plastic box (Tip 1) and leave to prove. This could take between 2–4 hours depending on the activity of your sour culture.
11. When fully proved (Tip 2) place the tray into your preheated oven and steam it. (How To 3).
12. Bake at 220°C (425°F) until golden brown (approximately 20–25 minutes).
13. Remove the tray from your oven and place the soup bowl loaves on a cooling wire rack.

The Breadcrust Bomb

The Breadcrust Bomb was inspired by a unique style of volcanic lava, which has a cracked and chequered exterior, resembling the surface of a loaf of bread.

I have tried to recreate this phenomenon within a sourdough to give a totally innovative and rather unusual four-layered loaf. The center contains turmeric-infused yellow wheat sour, the middle layer is a chilli-red wheat sour and the outer charcoal layer is made from a rye sour dough containing a blend of seeds and vegetable carbon. The exterior 'shell' is made from applying a unique black rye sour paste I have developed to recreate the Bomb's distinct brittle exterior. When you cut through it, it recreates the appearance of being molten lava in the center.

As you might sense, this is a multi-stage recipe that will take a little coordination to finally make this stunning loaf. You will need both active wheat and rye sour cultures ready to raise this loaf.

Makes: 1 large loaf

Stage 1—Make three different colored doughs
Although you won't be able to mix them at the same time it would be ideal to make them immediately one after the other. You can easily achieve this if everything is weighed before you start. The method of making each of the doughs will be the same. After which, when constructing the loaf, you should have approximately 140 g (5 oz) yellow center–260 g (9 ¼ oz) red middle layer–600 g (1 lb 5 oz) charcoal outer plus enough black rye sour paste to apply a thick layer just before baking.

Yellow Center (Dough 1)
70 g (2½ oz) strong white bread flour
1.5 g (pinch) salt
2.5 g (pinch) turmeric
30 g (1 oz) wheat sour culture, twice fed for three days
38 ml (1⅓ fl oz) water (tepid)

Red Middle (Dough 2)
140 g (5 oz) strong white bread flour
pinch salt
pinch hot chili powder
55 g (2 oz) wheat sour culture, twice fed for three days

68 ml (2½ fl oz) water (tepid)

*Red Paste Coloring added until a bright red color is achieved to the dough

Charcoal Outer (Dough 3)
295 g (10½ oz) strong white bread flour
5½ g (⅛ oz) salt
30 g (1 oz) multiseed blend (for example sunflower, millet, flax, poppy, pumpkin)
6 g (⅛ oz) mustard seeds
9 g (⅓ oz) vegetable carbon
120 g (4 oz) rye sour culture, twice fed for three days
150 ml (5 fl oz) water (tepid)

Stage 2—Black Rye Sour Paste Coating (make after all 3 doughs are made)

Ingredients
200 g (7 oz) rye sour culture, twice fed for three days
6 g (⅛ oz) caster (superfine) sugar
pinch of salt
20 g (⅔ oz) ground rice
8 g (⅓ oz) black onion seeds
14 g (¼ oz) black sesame seeds

14 g (¼ oz) black poppy seeds
10 g (⅓ oz) vegetable carbon
6 g (⅛ oz) vegetable oil
20 ml (1/8 fl oz) water (tepid)

Method

1. Weigh the dry ingredients separately then place them into three separate plastic bowls.

2. Prepare one dough at a time—add the sour culture, liquid and colors–combine together until a dough starts to form and the sides of the bowl are clean.

3. Remove dough from the bowl and knead (Technique 1) on your work surface until it becomes smooth and elastic (approximately 10–12 minutes). Use the windowpane test (Technique 3) to check if the dough is fully developed. You will note that the dough will take less time to become fully kneaded than a conventional yeasted dough.

4. Form the dough into a ball shape and place in a lidded plastic box and leave for 60 minutes.

5. Repeat this for the other two doughs. Try to do this quickly so that there is not too much time difference between the 3 doughs.

6. During your 1 hour break to allow the doughs to prove you will need to make the Black Rye Sour Paste Coating simply by stirring all the ingredients in a bowl and covering the bowl in plastic wrap or a shower cap.

7. After 60 minutes, remove the yellow dough from plastic box and gently stretch the dough and fold into three, press down, stretch and fold again into three against the way you first folded it. Repeat for the red and then the charcoal doughs.

8. Place the doughs back into their boxes and leave for a further 60 minutes.

9. Remove all three doughs from their plastic boxes and gently form each into a ball.

10. Place the doughs back in their plastic boxes, smooth side upwards, for 15 minutes to allow the doughs to relax.

11. Remove the yellow dough and gently re-round the ball.

12. Using a rolling pin, pin out the red dough into a square leaving the middle a little thicker (the square needs to be only just big enough to encase the yellow ball of dough).

13. Place yellow ball smooth side down onto the center of the red square of dough. Lift the four corners up so they meet in the middle and pinch them together to create a neat, even fit. Turn over so the join is now on the bottom and make into a ball shape with your hands.

14. Repeat this process again with the charcoal dough to encase the red dough. Aim to achieve a nice smooth dough on top and neatly sealed at the bottom.

15. Place onto a baking tray lined with baking paper generously sprinkled with ground rice or semolina.

16. Place into a covered plastic box (Tip 1) and leave to prove. This could take between 2–4 hours depending on the activity of your sour culture, but normally quicker than for the wheat sourdough.

17. When fully proved (Tip 2) generously, but carefully, paint on a thick layer of the black rye sour paste coating.

18. Sprinkle some ground rice/semolina on a pizza peel/pan or a flat, thin baking tray, then gently place the dough onto it.

19. Slide the dough onto your baking stone or heavy baking tray in your preheated oven and steam it. (How To 3).

20. Bake at 220°C (425°F) until a thick black crust is formed (approximately 35–40 minutes).

21. The nature of this loaf will mean it looks burnt throughout the entire baking time. If you make sure your oven temperature is correct and set a timer it should not leave the oven actually burnt.

22. Remove the baked loaf from your oven and place on a cooling wire rack.

Sweet Breads and Buns

Born out of a bread dough–but enriched with ingredients such as sugar, butter, egg, milk, fruits and spices-sweet, fermented buns are probably a baker's most attractive and indulgent everyday product. Many of the products within this category will be classics that have stood the test of time and some will be more modern, trendy products that look like they are here to stay. Within this selection of recipes is Cinnamon Square's signature product: The Cinnamon Square Bun. A sweet, fermented bun, rolled with a cinnamon filling and topped with a cream cheese frosting. A product so good it has won three UK national awards to date.

Posh Burger Buns

This recipe will make eight gourmet burger buns. You will require some top quality steak burgers to compliment these buns. They can be soft baked on a tray, but if you have Yorkshire pudding pans then your burger buns will have a deeper shape when baked. These trays are commonly found as an indented tray of four, approximately 10 cm (4 in) diameter. You will require some beaten egg and sesame seeds or mixed seeds (optional).

Makes: 8 gourmet burger buns

Ingredients

480 g (1 lb 1 oz) strong white bread flour
8.5 g (⅓ oz) salt
24 g (1 oz) caster (superfine) sugar
60 g (2 oz) white fat
10 g (¼ oz) fresh yeast OR 5 g (⅛ oz) dried yeast
260 ml (9 ¼ fl oz) water (tepid)

Method

1. Weigh all the dry ingredients separately, then place them in a plastic bowl, flour first then the rest in separate piles on top.

2. Add the water, and then combine together until a dough starts to form and the sides of the bowl are clean.

3. Remove the dough from the bowl and knead (Technique 1) on your work surface until it becomes smooth and elastic (approximately 12–15 minutes). Use the windowpane test (Technique 3) to check if the dough is fully developed.

4. Weigh 8 x 105 g (3½ oz) pieces, round them into ball shapes and place in a lidded plastic box and leave for 40 minutes.

5. Remove the balls from the plastic box and re-round.

6. Place back into the box and leave for a further 10 minutes.

7. Remove again from the box, and using a rolling pin gently roll the dough into circles slightly smaller than the indentation of the Yorkshire pudding tray or about 9 cm (3½ in) diameter if placing on a baking paper lined flat tray. Lightly grease the Yorkshire pudding tray by using a little white fat on a paper towel.

8. Place the tray(s) into a covered plastic box (Tip 1) and leave to prove for approximately 45–60 minutes.

9. When fully proved (Tip 2) gently brush the tops with beaten egg (or use a hand held water spray containing egg).

10. Either leave plain or sprinkle some sesame seeds on top of the egg, or alternatively try using a multiseed blend (for example, sunflower, millet, flax, poppy, pumpkin) to give a real posh look to them.

11. Place the tray(s) into your preheated oven and bake at 200°C (400°F) until golden brown (approximately 12–15 minutes).

12. Remove the tray(s) from your oven and place on a cooling wire rack.

TIP

Use the same process but instead of baking burger buns, roll them into finger buns; making them ideal for holding sausages.

Panettone

This recipe will make eight citrus-fresh, light and airy Panettone. You will find them so much moister than the longlife ones you find in the extravagant tins and boxes. You will need eight paper cases or ramekins about 7 cm (3 in) diameter. This dough will receive two periods of bulk fermentation and will start off as a firm dough, then turn to a sugary sticky dough and then end up as a silky soft dough. You will require some beaten egg and some flaked almonds for decoration.

Makes: 8 small Panettone

Stage 1

Ingredients
300 g (10½ oz) strong white bread flour
3 g (pinch) salt
20 g (¾ oz) fresh yeast OR 10 g (¼ oz) dried yeast
90 ml (3¼ fl oz) milk (room temperature)
75 g (2¾ oz) egg (room temperature)
vanilla extract, to taste

Method
1. Weigh all the dry ingredients separately, then place them in a plastic bowl, flour first then the rest in separate piles on top.
2. Add the milk and egg, and then combine together until a dough starts to form and the sides of the bowl are clean.
3. Remove the dough from the bowl and knead (Technique 1) on your work surface until it becomes smooth, but it will be very dry compared to most yeasted doughs (approximately 12–15 minutes).
4. Form the dough into a ball shape and place in a plastic bowl, cover with plastic wrap (or shower cap) and leave to bulk ferment (Fact 1) for 45 minutes.

Stage 2

Ingredients
60 g (2 oz) caster (superfine) sugar
30 g (1 oz) egg yolk (room temperature)
125 g (4½ oz) unsalted butter, softened

Method
1. Mix the caster (superfine) sugar and egg yolk together.
2. Add to the dough in the plastic bowl after its 45-minute bulk fermentation.
3. Start to work the liquid into the dough with your hand.
4. After it has come back to a dough, add the unsalted butter, softened and start to squeeze this into the dough.
5. After the butter is fully incorporated, place the very soft dough on your work surface and knead until it feels smooth and elastic, using the 'slapping' and 'stretching' action (Technique 4). It might take a while, but it will eventually get there. Use the windowpane test (Technique 3) to check if the dough is fully developed. It should feel soft, but silky smooth.
6. Form the dough into a ball shape and place in a plastic bowl, cover with plastic wrap (or shower cap) and leave to bulk ferment for a second 45 minutes.

Stage 3

Ingredients
150 g (5½ oz) sultanas
grated zest of 1 orange

Method
1. Add the sultanas and orange peel to the dough in the plastic bowl after its second 45-minute bulk fermentation.
2. Gently knead the ingredients into the dough until thoroughly blended in.
3. Weigh eight 100 g (3½ oz) pieces, shape them into balls and place into a lidded plastic box to rest for 10 minutes.
4. Re-round the balls and place them back into the lidded plastic box to rest for 10 minutes.

5. Remove from the plastic box, re-round again and place into your paper cases or lightly-greased ramekins of approximately 7 cm (3 in) diameter with the smooth side of the dough facing upwards.

6. Place on a baking tray and leave to prove in the lidded plastic box for 45–60 minutes.

7. When fully proved (Tip 2), gently paint the top of each

ball with beaten egg and sprinkle a few flaked almonds on the top of each ball.

8. Place in your oven and bake at 180°C (350°F) until a rich, golden brown color (approximately 15–20 minutes).

9. Remove the baked panettone from your oven and place on a cooling wire rack.

Sweet Breads and Buns

Swiss (Finger) Buns

Another longtime classic sweet, fermented bun, commonplace in most traditional baker's shops. These are so simple but totally irresistible once you have made them. Although it is normal to finish with a simple fondant iced top, there is no reason why you cannot get really carried away by adding fillings such as cream, jams, curds or ganache and then toppings including chocolate fudge, nuts, sprinkles or even a feathering decoration too. They just get even more irresistible! The recipe is based on the one used to make the Chelsea bun dough.

Makes: 10 Swiss (Finger) Buns

Ingredients
435 g (15½ oz) strong white bread flour
2 pinches of salt
50 g (1¾ oz) unsalted butter, softened
50 g (1¾ oz) caster (superfine) sugar
28 g (1 oz) fresh yeast OR 10 g (¼ oz) of dried yeast
34 g (1¼ oz) egg (room temperature)
77 ml (2¾ fl oz) water (tepid)
125 ml (4½ fl oz) semi-skimmed milk

Method
1. You will also need some Fondant Icing (Fillings and Toppings page 190) for decoration.
2. Weigh all the dry ingredients separately, then place them in a plastic bowl, flour first then the rest in separate piles on top including the unsalted butter, softened.
3. Add the egg, water and milk, and then combine together until a dough starts to form and the sides of the bowl are clean.
4. Remove the dough from the bowl and knead (Technique 1) on your work surface until it becomes smooth and elastic (approximately 12–15 minutes). Expect the dough to feel soft and sticky for the first few minutes of the kneading process.
5. Use the windowpane test (Technique 3) to check if the dough is fully developed.
6. Weigh the dough into ten 75 g (2¾ oz) ball shapes and place them in a lidded plastic box and leave to bulk ferment (Fact 1) for 50 minutes.
7. Remove the balls from the plastic box and re-round.

8. Place them back into the box and leave for a further 10 minutes.
9. Remove them from the plastic box and elongate, by rolling under your hand into sausage shapes, each approximately 10 cm (4 in) long.
10. Place each one on a baking tray lined with baking paper leaving space around each one to grow whilst proving and also whilst baking in the oven, without touching.
11. Place the tray into a lidded plastic box and leave to prove for approximately 45 minutes.
12. When fully proved (Tip 2), remove the tray from the box and bake at 220°C (425°F) for 10–12 minutes. The buns will be golden brown and will soften as they cool down.
13. Remove the tray from your oven and place on a cooling wire rack.
14. When cool dip the top of bun in Fondant Icing (Fillings and Toppings page 190) (which can be colored and flavored). When the icing is set, you can gently cut in half and then add your chosen fillings.

Hot Cross Buns

These lightly-spiced fruited buns with the traditional cross on the top make for a real Easter time favorite. In the bakery for the weeks leading up to Easter we would be making hundreds daily then on Good Friday we would have hot cross buns literally everywhere! Personally, I recommend toasting them and applying some butter before eating them. The cross is said to let the devil out and expel bad spirits.

Makes: 9 Hot Cross Buns

Stage 1— Dough

Ingredients
350 g (12 oz) strong white bread flour
5.5 g (⅕ oz) salt
53 g (2 oz) caster (superfine) sugar
5 g (⅕ oz) cinnamon
5 g (⅕ oz) mixed spice
2.5 g (pinch) nutmeg
53 g (2 oz) unsalted butter, softened
27 g (1 oz) fresh yeast OR 15 g (½ oz) of dried yeast
27 g (1 oz) egg (room temperature)
155 ml (5½ fl oz) water (tepid)
53 g (2 oz) currants (washed and drained)
53 g (2 oz) sultanas (washed and drained)

Method
1. Weigh all the dry ingredients separately, then place them in a plastic bowl, flour first then the rest in separate piles on top, including the butter.
2. Add the egg, water and milk, then combine together until a dough starts to form and the sides of the bowl are clean.
3. Remove the dough from the bowl and knead (Technique 1) on your work surface until it becomes smooth and elastic (approximately 12–15 minutes). Expect the dough to feel soft and sticky for the first few minutes of the kneading process.
4. Use the windowpane test (Technique 3) to check if the dough is fully developed.
5. Flatten the dough, sprinkle a layer of currants and sultanas over the surface, roll up the dough and gently knead to start evenly distributing them within the dough, trying not to damage the dried fruit too much as sugar within them will come out and cause the buns to bake very dark.
6. Weigh the dough into nine 85 g (3 oz) pieces and shape them into balls and place in a lidded plastic box and leave to bulk ferment (Fact 1) for 50 minutes.
7. Remove the balls from the plastic box and re-round.
8. Place them back into the box and leave for a further 10 minutes.
9. Remove again from the plastic box and gently re-round again. Place each ball on a baking tray lined with baking paper, leaving space around each one to grow whilst proving and whilst baking in the oven without touching. They can be a little closer so they actually do touch, which gives a softer bake to the sides due to sticking together.
10. Place the tray into a lidded plastic box and leave to prove for approximately 45 minutes.
11. Whilst proving, it is the ideal time to make the crossing mix.
12. When fully proved (Tip 2), remove the tray from the box and gently paint the top of each ball with beaten egg.
13. Pipe the crossing mix over the buns. Try piping in straight lines. For example, if laid out 3 x 3 buns on the tray, pipe three horizontal lines then pipe three vertical lines (only stopping when you get to the end of each line).
14. Place the tray into your preheated oven and bake at 220°C (425°F) for 12–15 minutes until golden brown.
15. Remove the tray from your oven and place on a cooling wire rack.

16. Stage 2—Crossing Mixture

Ingredients
150 g (5½ oz) strong white bread flour
30 g (1 oz) white fat
150 ml (5½ fl oz) water (tepid)

Method
17. Weigh all the dry ingredients separately, then place them in a plastic bowl, flour first then the white fat on top.
18. Using your fingers, rub the fat into the flour until no lumps can be seen.
19. Add the water, and then mix with a wooden spoon until a smooth batter is formed.
20. Place in a plastic piping bag and cut a 3–5 mm (¼ in) hole in the end.

TIP

Add the grated zest of an orange and a lemon to give the buns a citrus note.

PAUL'S TOP TIP

Use a strong sandwich bag and cut a small hole 3–5 mm (¼ in maximum) in the bottom corner to use a piping bag as an alternative. Start with a very small hole and practice piping straight lines on the work surface (you can scrape this back into the back and re-pipe). You can always increase the size of the hole if it is too small.

Chelsea Buns

A real longtime classic, sweet, fermented bun with a fruit filling—commonplace in most traditional baker's shops. You will require a 22.5 cm (9 in) square baking pan.

Makes: 4 Chelsea Buns

Ingredients

Chelsea Bun Filling
100 g (3½ oz) raw (demerara) sugar
50 g (1¾ oz) unsalted butter, softened
Combine both ingredients in a bowl with a spoon until thoroughly mixed together.

Chelsea Bun Dried Fruits Mixture
100 g (3½ oz) currants (pre-soaked and drained)
25 g (1 oz) mixed peel

Dough
310 g (11 oz) strong white bread flour
3 g (pinch) salt
35 g (1⅕ oz) caster (superfine) sugar
20 g (⅔ oz) fresh yeast OR 10 g (¼ oz) of dried yeast
35 g (1⅕ oz) unsalted butter, softened
24 g (1 oz) egg (room temperature)
55 ml (2 fl oz) water (tepid)
90 ml (3⅕ fl oz) semi-skimmed milk (lukewarm)

Method

1. To make filling: Combine the currants and mixed peel until thoroughly mixed together.

2. To make dough: You will also need some beaten egg and raw sugar for decoration.

3. Weigh all the dry ingredients separately, then place them in a plastic bowl, flour first then the rest in separate piles on top including the softened, unsalted butter.

4. Add the egg, water and milk, and then combine together until a dough starts to form and the sides of the bowl are clean.

5. Remove the dough from the bowl and knead (Technique 1) on your work surface until it becomes smooth and elastic (approximately 12–15 minutes). Expect the dough to feel soft and sticky for the first few minutes of the kneading process.

6. Use the windowpane test (Technique 3) to check if the dough is fully developed.

7. Form the dough into a sausage/cylinder shape and place in a lidded plastic box and leave to bulk ferment (Fact 1) for 50 minutes.

8. Remove the fermented dough from the box and, using a rolling pin, roll the dough to a rectangle 20 cm (8 in) high x 35 cm (14 in) wide.

9. Rotate the dough so it is positioned with the 20 cm (8 in) edge closest to you.

10. Using a pallet knife, spread the Chelsea bun filling over the dough, leaving the edge closest to you free from any filling.

11. Sprinkle the Chelsea bun dried fruits mixture over the top and lightly press into the Chelsea bun filling.

12. Press the edge closest to you flat and lightly spray with water.

13. Starting from the end furthest from you, roll up to an even thickness sausage of 20 cm (8 in) long.

14. Using a long, sharp serrated knife cut four 5 cm (2 in) buns (use a sawing action to prevent squashing the rolled dough pieces).

15. Place buns, swirl side up, into a baking paper lined 23 cm (9 in) square baking tin.

16. Brush the top of each bun with beaten egg.

17. Place in a lidded plastic tub to prove for approximately 45 minutes.

18. When fully proved (Tip 2), remove from the plastic tub, Place the pastry cases on a baking tray and bake at 220°C (425°F) for 8–12 minutes. Look down between the buns to check that they are not raw at the bottom.

19. Remove the tray of buns from your oven and immediately sprinkle with raw sugar.

20. Place on a cooling wire rack.

Tea Cakes

A pot of tea and a toasted tea cake makes for a lovely start to the day. Made from a rich buttery yeasted dough and packed with dried fruits. When baked, the tea cakes are best served cut in two, toasted and smothered in butter.

Makes: 8 tea cakes

Ingredients

400 g (14 oz) strong white bread flour
pinch of salt
70 g (2½ oz) caster (superfine) sugar
30 g (1 oz) fresh yeast OR 15 g (½ oz) of dried yeast
100 ml (3½ fl oz) milk (room temperature)
100 ml (3½ fl oz) water (tepid)
70 g (2½ oz) unsalted butter, softened
100 g (3½ oz) currants (washed and drained)
100 g (3½ oz) sultanas (washed and drained)
20 g (⅔ oz) mixed peel

Method

1. Weigh all the dry ingredients separately, then place them in a plastic bowl, flour first then the salt, sugar and yeast in separate piles on top.
2. Add the milk and water, and then combine together until a dough starts to form and the sides of the bowl are clean.
3. Remove the dough from the bowl and knead (Technique 1) on your work surface until it becomes smooth and elastic (approximately 12–15 minutes). Expect the dough to feel firm as you knead. When the butter is added it will then become soft.
4. Use the windowpane test (Technique 3) to check if the dough is fully developed.
5. Place the dough back into your plastic bowl then add the butter. Using one hand; start squeezing the butter into the dough. It might take a little while but keep persevering.
6. After the butter is fully incorporated, place the dough on your work surface and knead until it feels smooth and elastic.

7. Flatten the dough, sprinkle a layer of currants, sultanas and mixed peel over the surface, roll up the dough and gently knead to start evenly distributing them within the dough, trying not to damage the dried fruit too much as sugar within them will come out and cause the tea cakes to bake very dark.
8. Weigh the dough into eight 125 g (4½ oz) pieces, shape them into balls and place them in a lidded plastic box and leave to bulk ferment (Fact 1) for 50 minutes.
9. Remove the balls from the plastic box and re-round.
10. Place them back into the box and leave for a further 10 minutes.
11. Remove again from the plastic box and, using a rolling pin, gently roll the balls into approximately 12.5 cm (5 in) discs.
12. Place each one on a baking paper lined baking tray, leaving space around each one to grow whilst proving and whilst baking in the oven without touching. Depending on the size of your tray, you might need two trays.
13. Place tray(s) into a lidded plastic box and leave to prove for approximately 45 minutes.
14. When fully proved (Tip 2), remove the tray(s) from the box, place in your oven and bake at 220°C (425°F) for 12–15 minutes until golden brown.
15. Remove the tray from your oven and place on a cooling wire rack.
16. Best served cut in half, toasted and finished with a layer of butter spread over each half.

Brioche

A sweet, fermented dough that is extremely rich in butter and egg. This recipe has chocolate chips included but you can omit them from the recipe if you prefer not to use them. You will require two small bread tins, lined with baking paper.

Makes: 2 small loaves

Ingredients

400 g (14 oz) strong white bread flour
6 g (¼ oz) salt
40 g (1½ oz) caster (superfine) sugar
20 g (⅔ oz) fresh yeast OR 10 g (¼ oz) of dried yeast
105 ml (3½ fl oz) milk (room temperature)
120 g (4¼ oz) egg (room temperature)
120 g (4¼ oz) unsalted butter, softened
100 g (3½ oz) dark chocolate chips (optional)

Method

1. Weigh all the dry ingredients separately, then place them in a plastic bowl, flour first then the salt, sugar and yeast in separate piles on top.

2. Add the milk and egg, and then combine together until a dough starts to form and the sides of the bowl are clean.

3. Remove the dough from the bowl and knead (Technique 1) on your work surface until it becomes smooth and elastic (approximately 12–15 minutes). Expect the dough to feel firm but slightly sticky as you knead. After the butter is added later it will then become soft.

4. Use the windowpane test (Technique 3) to check if the dough is fully developed.

5. Place the dough back in your plastic bowl and then add the butter. Using one hand; start squeezing the butter into the dough. It might take a little while but keep persevering.

6. After the butter is fully incorporated, place the very soft dough on your work surface and knead until it feels smooth and elastic, using the dough using the 'slapping' and 'stretching' action (Technique 4) It might take a while, but it will eventually get there. For a second time, use the windowpane test (Technique 3) to check if the dough is fully developed.

7. Flatten the dough, sprinkle a layer of chocolate chips over the surface, roll up the dough and gently knead to start evenly distributing them within the dough. Try not to be too aggressive as it will cause the dough to stain a grey color from the chocolate.

8. Weigh two 450 g (1 lb) pieces, round them into ball shapes, place in a lidded plastic box and leave to bulk ferment (Fact 1) for 50 minutes. If you do not choose to add chocolate chips the dough pieces will weigh 400 g (14 oz) each.

9. Remove the fermented dough balls from the plastic box and re-round.

10. Place back into the box and leave for a further 10 minutes.

11. Remove the balls from the box and shape the dough to form a sausage/cylinder (Technique 2)—the same length as the length of tin to be used.

12. Place in a lidded plastic tub to prove for approximately 45 minutes.

13. When fully proved (Tip 2), remove the tins from the box, place in your oven and bake at 220°C (425°F) for 20 minutes. The brioche loaves should be dark brown on top and golden on the sides.

14. Allow to cool in the tin for 30 minutes before removing.

TIP

Have a plastic bowl scraper to hand when working with the soft dough on the table. You will find this useful to gather up the dough as you are working with it, until the dough becomes more bound together. You will also find it ideal for scraping your hands clean too!

Cinnamon Square Buns

Born out of my trips to America and Canada, the Cinnamon Square Bun has become our signature product. A sweet, fermented bun, rolled with a cinnamon filling and topped with a cream cheese frosting has become a real winner at Cinnamon Square. In fact, it has won four national UK awards to date.

Although cinnamon buns are lovely to eat at room temperature, I would always recommend eating them warm, either soon after they leave the oven or, if reheated, it is best to do this in the microwave as they stay soft and gooey. If you prefer to heat them in a conventional oven then place some foil over the top to prevent the cream cheese frosting from burning and the buns from drying out.

Makes: 4 large buns

Stage 1—Cinnamon Bun Filling

Ingredients
100 g (3½ oz) caster (superfine) sugar
50 g (1¾ oz) unsalted butter, softened
10 g (¼ oz) ground cinnamon

Method
1. Combine ingredients in a bowl with a spoon until thoroughly mixed together.

Stage 2—Cream Cheese Frosting

Ingredients
50 g (1¾ oz) cream cheese
125 g (4½ oz) icing (confectioners') sugar
15 g (½ oz) unsalted butter, softened

Method
1. Combine ingredients in a bowl with a spoon until thoroughly mixed together. Do not over mix as the frosting will soften too much.

Stage 3—Dough

Ingredients
300 g (10½ oz) strong white bread flour
25 g (1 oz) caster (superfine) sugar
5 g (1/6 oz) salt
10 g (¼ oz) fresh yeast OR 5 g (1/6 oz) of dried yeast
100 ml (3½ fl oz) milk (room temperature)
50 ml (1¾ fl oz) water (tepid)
25 g (1 oz) unsalted butter, softened

Method
2. Weigh all the dry ingredients separately, then place them in a plastic bowl, flour first then the salt, sugar and yeast in separate piles on top.
3. Add the milk and water, and then combine together until a dough starts to form and the sides of the bowl are clean.
4. Remove the dough from the bowl and knead (Technique 1) on your work surface until it becomes smooth and elastic (approximately 12–15 minutes). Expect the dough to feel firm as you knead. When the butter is added later, it will then become soft.
5. Use the windowpane test (Technique 3) to check if the dough is fully developed.
6. Place the dough back in your plastic bowl then add the butter. Using one hand; start squeezing the butter into the dough. It might take a little while but keep persevering.
7. After the butter is fully incorporated, place the dough on your work surface and knead until it feels smooth and elastic.
8. Form the dough into a sausage/cylinder shape and place in a lidded plastic box and leave to bulk ferment

(Fact 1) for 50 minutes.

9. Remove the fermented dough from the box and, using a rolling pin, roll the dough to a rectangle 20 cm (8 in) high x 35 cm (14 in) wide.

10. Rotate the dough with the 20 cm (8 in) edge closest to you.

11. Using a pallet knife, spread the cinnamon bun filling over the dough, leaving the edge closest to you free from any filling.

12. Press the edge closest to you flat and lightly spray with water.

13. Starting from the end furthest from you, roll up to an even thickness sausage of 20 cm (8 in) long.

14. Using along, sharp serrated knife cut 4 x 5 cm (2 in) buns (use a sawing action to prevent squashing the rolled dough pieces).

15. Place buns, swirl side up, into a baking paper lined 22.5 cm (9 in) square baking tin.

16. Place in a lidded plastic tub to prove for approximately 45 minutes.

17. When fully proved (Tip 2), remove from the box and bake at 220°C (425°F) for 8–12 minutes.

18. Remove the tray from the oven and place on a cooling wire rack to coll for 10 minutes.

19. Spread the cream cheese frosting over the buns. The frosting should soften a little and run into the buns, but at the same time leaving a nice layer on top.

20. They are now ready to eat, warm and gooey!

TIP

You can freeze the whole tray with the topping on. Make sure they are cut before freezing and then you can take one out at a time.

Cakes and Sponges

Who can say no to a slice of Victoria Sandwich or Swiss roll? I know I can't. But did you know one is a cake and the other a sponge? Do you know what the difference is between a cake and a sponge? I find today the terms are used so loosely that they have lost their real meaning. If I go back to my old baking books there are chapters on cakes and chapters on sponges, so I need to highlight the fundamental original differences here as I will refer to the recipes in this chapter as how they were classically defined.

As far as the ingredients go, they both contain sugar, egg, flour (with baking powder added or it is added separately, although not all sponges have baking powder). The fundamental difference is the inclusion of fat in a cake, coming from adding butter, margarine, oil or white fat to the recipe. Therefore a sponge will be very light and will stale quickly and is generally used for gâteaux, tortes and Swiss rolls. Whereas cake will be heavier textured, tender to eat and will have a much longer shelf life.

Their methods of manufacture are very different too. A sponge is made by whisking eggs and sugar into a foam like a meringue, and then the flour is gently folded through the fragile foam. For a cake, sugar and butter are beaten until a light textured cream is formed. egg is gradually incorporated and then flour (containing baking powder or added separately) is thoroughly mixed in to create a heavy batter (in comparison to that of a sponge).

There are other methods for making cakes and sponges, but the two methods I have described simplify the fundamental differences. You will also come across recipes that are basically hybrids of the two; an enriched sponge with added melted butter for example. So then it begs the question, when does a sponge become a cake?

There are some wonderful tried and tested recipes in this section for you to bake, but which one will try first?

Swiss Roll

A true bakery classic and the best recipe to learn the required technique for making sponges. The critical stages are:

- achieving a thick foam
- incorporating the flour without the foam collapsing
- rolling the sponge without cracks appearing.

Makes: 1 Swiss roll sheet approximately 36 cm x 25 cm (14¼ in x 10 in)

Ingredients

300 g (10½ oz) egg (room temperature)
100 g (3½ oz) caster (superfine) sugar
100 g (3½ oz) plain (all purpose) flour
Extra caster (superfine) sugar and a jar of strawberry jam are needed for finishing Swiss roll.

Method

1. Place the eggs and sugar into a grease-free plastic bowl and whisk together until a thick foam is formed; the ribbon stage (Technique 5).

2. Place the flour in a sieve.

3. Lightly sift a layer of flour on top of the batter and, using the whisk, gently fold the batter over the flour, and then sift a little more flour on top. Keep repeating this until all the flour is added. It is vital this is carried out gently to prevent breaking down the foam back to a liquid.

4. Once all the flour is incorporated and no lumps can be seen, refrain from any further mixing of the batter.

5. Line your Swiss roll tray with baking paper.

6. Starting from one end, gently pour the batter towards the other end. Let the batter make its own level. Gently push the batter into the corners so the tray is evenly full of batter.

7. Bake at 200°C (400°F) for 6–8 minutes. It should be golden brown when baked.

8. Whilst the Swiss roll is baking, place a sheet of baking paper (a little larger than the Swiss roll tray) on your work surface and sprinkle a layer of caster (superfine) sugar on top.

9. When baked, invert the tray and lay the Swiss roll face down onto the sugared paper. Remove the tray and leave the sponge to cool down with the paper still attached to the bottom (which is now facing upwards).

10. After approximately 15 minutes it should have cooled sufficiently enough to finish.

11. Starting from one corner, gently peel away the baking paper and discard.

12. Position the Swiss roll (still on the sugared paper) in landscape orientation.

13. Spread on a layer of jam, leaving a 1 cm (½ in) un-jammed strip at the top and bottom edges.

14. Press flat, the edge closest to you. This will be the finishing edge once rolled up.

15. Starting from the edge furthest from you, fold over and press tight (this will help prevent a large hole through the middle). Repeat this again.

16. Lift the sugared paper furthest away with both hands and pull towards you trapping the sponge and encouraging it to roll rather than slide. Try not to be too heavy-handed as the jam will be squeezed out.

17. When completely rolled up, leave to stand with the final end joint underneath as this will prevent it from unrolling.

18. Finish with a generous sprinkling of caster (superfine) sugar and then cut into slices. This Swiss roll is best eaten on the day it is made.

TIPS

* To help retain moisture in any of the cakes, add glycerine at 20 g per kg (³/₄ oz per 2 lb 4 oz) of cake batter.
* Make sure the eggs are at least room temperature for making cakes and sponges. eggs contain lecithin which is an emulsifier. Lecithin will aid aeration and does this more effectively if the eggs are not cold. For sponges, where you are whisking eggs to form a foam, you can do this over a bowl of hot water. I aim for a foam temperature of 25°C (77°F) to get the best out of your eggs.

PAUL'S TOP TIP

To prevent cakes and sponges from sitting back or dipping in the center after baking you need to drop or bang the tin as you remove it from the oven. Yes, bang the tin! It might sound the last thing you would wish to do to such a delicate product but it does actually prevent any collapsing occurring. Drop it from about 30 cm (12 in) onto a hard level surface. You might well see steam expelled from the cake or sponge, this is a good thing.

Sponge Sandwich

Using the same whisking principle as for making a Swiss roll, the sponge sandwich is also not a cake, and therefore no fat is present in the recipe. However the recipe differs to the Swiss roll as a lot less egg is used, leaving more flour present to impart structure and strength for the sandwich to stand up. In the Swiss roll, the extra egg allows the baked sponge to roll up without cracking, but if this recipe was used to make a sandwich it would collapse back on itself. Most bakeries would use a pre-mix to make their sponges, or they would add an emulsifier (E471—Mono—and diglycerides of fatty acids to their scratch recipe) to improve the batter stability, impart a finer crumb structure and increase the softness and shelf life.

A sponge sandwich can be cut in two, filled with jam or fresh fruits, and a layer of whipped fresh cream. The top can be simply dusted with icing (confectioners') sugar or a layer of fondant icing can be spread on, which can also be colored and flavored to compliment the chosen filling. I remember in my youthful baking days making coffee-flavored fondant topped sponge sandwiches filled with freshly-whipped cream.

This recipe makes two sponges, which can either be cut in half and filled, or if you want to make a more chunky decorated sponge then place one on top of the other (the bottom layer might require the top levelling off first before adding your choice of fillings).

Makes: two 20 cm (8 in) round sponges

Ingredients
210 g (7½ oz) egg (room temperature)
145 g (5 oz) caster (superfine) sugar
145 g (5 oz) plain (all purpose) flour
Depending on your choice of finish, you might require
    55 g (2 oz) jam or 140 g (5 oz) whipped fresh cream per
    sponge sandwich.

Method
1. Place the eggs and sugar into a grease-free plastic bowl and whisk together until a thick foam is formed; the ribbon stage (Technique 5).
    Mixing Tip: Add 8 g (¼ oz) Glycerine to the foam once whisked (before adding flour), to help keep the baked sponge soft for a little longer.
2. Blend through the optional glycerine if used.
3. Place the flour in a sieve.
4. Lightly sift a layer of flour on top of the batter and, using the whisk, gently fold the batter over the flour, and then sift a little more flour on top. Keep repeating this until all the flour is added. It is vital this is carried out gently to

prevent breaking down the foam back to a liquid.
5. Once all the flour is incorporated and no lumps can be seen, refrain from any further mixing of the batter.
6. Line the base of your cake pans with a disc of baking paper and coat the sides in a layer of white fat.
7. Slowly pour 225 g (8 oz) sponge batter into each cake pan and gently spread level.
8. Place the sponges in your oven and bake at 180°C (350°F) for 20–25 minutes. It should be golden brown when baked.
    Baking Tip: The sponge is fully baked if no marks remain after drawing your fingers lightly across the top surface.
9. When baked, remove from your oven and immediately turn out onto a cooling wire rack (leave to cool upside-down).
10. When cool, cut in half horizontally (Technique 7).
11. If covering the top with fondant do that first. Refer to the Fondant recipe options (page 190).
12. Place the bottom layer on a plate and then add your choice of fillings.
13. Place your top layer on and serve.

Victoria Sandwich

As the Swiss roll is the best recipe to learn to make sponges, the Victoria Sandwich is by far the best recipe to learn the fundamentals of cake making. Containing equal amounts of butter, sugar, eggs and flour (and a raising agent) it stretches those ingredients to the maximum, so much so that it is thwart with failure for the untrained. By following my advice on the critical stages of this recipe you should achieve the perfect cake every time. The method you will use to make this cake is called the 'sugar batter' method.

The Victoria Sandwich, albeit simply finished, is one of the nicest cakes you can make. And, like a scone filled with clotted cream and jam, it is ever-present in an afternoon tea selection.

Makes: one 23 cm (9 in) round cake

Ingredients
250 g (9 oz) unsalted butter, softened
250 g (9 oz) caster (superfine) sugar
250 g (9 oz) egg (room temperature)
250 g (9 oz) self-raising (self-rising) flour
200 g (7 oz) strawberry jam
500 g (1 lb 2 oz) buttercream (page 200)
Extra icing (confectioners') sugar is required for finishing
  the Victoria Sandwich.

Preferably use a loose-bottom 23 cm (9 in) round cake pan.

Method
1. Place the butter and sugar into a grease-free plastic bowl and beat together with a wooden spoon until light and fluffy. Please refer to the Quality Control Section (page 222)

2. Next the egg is added a bit at a time. Add in at least six separate additions, or many more if you like. If the egg is added too quickly, the batter will curdle. After each addition of egg is incorporated, beat it well before adding the next portion of egg. If you find any signs of water droplets appearing on the batter before all the egg is added, stop adding any more egg and add all the flour as described below then add the remaining egg once the flour has been mixed in. By doing this you will retain the batter in the best condition and cause minimal detriment to the potential baked height of the cake.

3. Add the flour to the batter and mix thoroughly to make sure there are no lumps or areas of the batter that have no flour (you can see these as they will be darker in color to that which has the flour incorporated). You can be heavy-handed with this as you are not going to deflate the batter or toughen the cake. Scrape down the sides of the bowl and give one final mix.

4. Line the bottom of the inside of your baking pan with a disc of baking paper and coat the sides in a thin layer of white fat or non-stick spray if you have some.

5. Place the batter in the center of the pan and spread to form an even layer, trying not to get batter up the sides of the pan which will burn.

6. Place the pan into your oven on the lower shelf and bake at 170°C (325°F) for 40 minutes or so. It should be golden brown when baked and springy in the center (Technique 6).

7. When baked, remove from your oven, bang the pan and leave in the baking pan to cool down.

8. Remove the cake from the baking pan and cut in half horizontally (Technique 7).

9. Spread a generous layer of jam on the top of the bottom half.

10. Spread a generous layer of buttercream on the cut surface of the top layer.

11. Carefully place the top layer back on the cake.

12. Using icing (confectioners') sugar in a fine sieve; dust the top of the cake.

13. Place in the fridge to firm up before cutting slices (generally eight portions from a 23 cm (9 in) round cake) otherwise the cake slides as you cut through.

Chocolate Cake

This recipe makes a really good chocolate cake base that can be sandwiched with ganache and chocolate buttercream, or it can be used as a celebration cake and covered in sugar paste.

Makes: one 23 cm (9 in) round cake

Ingredients
200 g (7 oz) self-raising (self-rising) flour
200 g (7 oz) unsalted butter, softened
200 g (7 oz) caster (superfine) sugar
12 g (¼ oz) baking powder
330 g (11½ oz) egg (room temperature)
60 g (2 oz) unsweetened cocoa powder
200 g (7 oz) milk chocolate ganache (page 212)
500 g (1 lb 2 oz) chocolate buttercream (page 200)

Extra icing (confectioners') sugar and unsweetened cocoa powder is required for finishing the chocolate cake.

Method
1. Place the flour, butter, sugar and baking powder in a bowl and beat together with a wooden spoon until a paste.
2. In a separate bowl, whisk the eggs and cocoa powder together, breaking down any lumps.
3. Gradually add the liquid to the paste, mixing all the time until all the liquid is added. Then mix for a couple of minutes, making sure the sides of the bowl are scraped down.
4. Line the bottom of the inside of your baking pan with a disc of baking paper and coat the sides in a thin layer of white fat or non-stick spray if you have some.
5. Place the batter in the center of the pan and spread to form an even layer, trying not to get batter up the sides of the pan, which will burn.
6. Place the pan into your oven on the lower shelf and bake at 170°C (325°F) for 40 minutes or so. It will be difficult to judge by color alone when baked but it will be springy in the center (Technique 6).
7. When baked, remove from your oven, bang the pan and leave in the baking pan to cool down.
8. Remove the cake from baking pan and cut in half horizontally (Technique 7).
9. Spread a generous layer of ganache on the top of the bottom half.
10. Spread a generous layer of chocolate buttercream on the cut surface of the top layer.
11. Carefully place the top layer back on the cake.
12. Using icing (confectioners') sugar mixed with some cocoa powder in a fine sieve, dust the top of the cake.
13. Place in the fridge to firm up before cutting slices (generally eight portions from a 23 cm (9 in) round cake) otherwise it slides as you cut through.

TIP

Place the cake in the fridge once baked and cool. This will firm up the cake and make the cutting in half procedure easier. Never try cutting the cake if frozen.

Carrot Cake

Cakes containing vegetables have been popular for many years and this has to be the most common version of them all. The use of vegetables adds lots of moisture to the cake, which can be detrimental to the cake by imparting a stodgy texture. Therefore using the correct weight of the vegetables is important and a longer bake is helpful too.

Makes: one 23 cm (9 in) round cake

Ingredients
100 g (3½ oz) unsalted butter, softened
200 g (7 oz) raw (demerara) sugar
100 g (3½ oz) egg (room temperature)
200 g (7 oz) cake flour (or plain (all purpose) flour)
2 g (pinch) mixed spice
2 pinches of cinnamon
14 g (1/4 oz) cornflour (cornstarch)
6 g (⅛ oz) baking powder
2.5 g (pinch) bicarbonate of soda
160 g (5½ oz) grated carrots
70 g (2½ oz) walnuts (chopped)
90 g (3⅕ oz) natural yogurt
350 g (12 oz) Cream Cheese Frosting (make half the recipe on page 202)
Chopped walnuts for sprinkling over the top.

Method
1. Place butter and sugar into a grease-free plastic bowl and beat together with a wooden spoon until 'light' and 'fluffy' (see page 222). Although bear in mind this mixture will be a little darker due to the raw sugar.

2. Next the egg is added a bit at a time. Add in at least six separate additions, or many more if you like. If the egg is added too quickly, the batter will curdle. After each addition of egg is incorporated, beat it well before adding the next portion of egg. If you find any signs of water droplets appearing on the batter before all the egg is added, stop adding any more egg and add the flour as described below, and then add the remaining egg once all the flour has been mixed in. By doing this you will retain the batter in the best condition and cause minimal detriment to the potential baked height of the cake.

3. Add the flour, spices, cornflour (cornstarch), baking powder and bicarbonate of soda to the batter and mix thoroughly to make sure there are no lumps or areas of the batter which have no flour (you can see these as they will be darker in color to that which has the flour incorporated). You can be heavy-handed with this as you are not going to deflate the batter or toughen the cake.

4. Finally add the grated carrots, chopped walnuts and yogurt and blend through until thoroughly mixed.

5. Line the bottom of the inside of your baking pan with a disc of baking paper and coat the sides in a thin layer of white fat or non-stick spray if you have some.

6. Place the batter in the center of the pan and spread to form an even layer, trying not to get batter up the sides of the pan, which will burn.

7. Place the cake pan in your oven on the lower shelf and bake at 170°C (325°F) for 40 minutes or so. It should be golden brown when baked and springy in the center (Technique 6).

8. When baked, remove the cake from your oven, bang the pan and leave in the baking pan to cool down.

9. Remove the carrot cake from baking pan and spread a generous layer of cream cheese frosting over the top.

10. Sprinkle some finely chopped walnuts onto the cream cheese frosting.

11. Place the cake in the fridge to firm up before cutting slices (generally eight portions from a 23 cm (9 in) round cake).

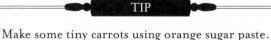

TIP

Make some tiny carrots using orange sugar paste. Roll small pieces into a pointed carrot and then you can add a tiny piece of green for the top of the carrot. Make one for the top of each slice.

Brownie (gluten-free)

What's not to like about a Belgian chocolate brownie? Served warm or ambient, it's equally delicious. Although this is a cake, it requires a completely different method compared to the sugar batter method as used for the Victoria Sandwich. What is also unique to the brownie is the small amount of flour that is used, therefore it makes the ideal recipe to convert to gluten-free, and this recipe is. If you prefer, you can use plain (all purpose) flour.

Makes: 9 brownies

Ingredients
210 g (7½ oz) unsalted butter
210 g (7½ oz) dark Belgian chocolate
285 g (10 oz) caster (superfine) sugar
170 g (6 oz) egg (room temperature)
125 g (4½ oz) gluten-free plain (all purpose) flour

Method
1. Place the butter and chocolate in a plastic bowl and gently melt them in the microwave or over a hot water bath. After they have melted, raise the temperature until they are warm, approximately 50°C (122°F). This will help keep the batter fluid when adding the eggs.

2. In a separate bowl combine the sugar and eggs together, and then pour (whilst stirring) into the butter/chocolate mixture.

3. Finally, add the gluten-free flour and stir until thoroughly combined.

4. Pour the mixture into your baking paper lined 23 cm (9 in) square baking pan. If the batter is still warm, it will make its own level. However if the batter has thickened, you will need to spread it level across the baking pan.

5. Place the pan into your oven and bake at 170°C (325°F) for 25–30 minutes. This is one cake where you actually want the center to still be slightly soft when baked.

6. Brownie can be eaten soon after baking or allowed to cool, then decorated with melted chocolate or chocolate fudge, then cut into nine pieces (7.5 cm (3 in) squares).

Red Velvet Cake

After the recent importation of this trend from the USA, it has become a firm favorite in the UK now. Generally made into whole cakes or cupcakes, it contains vinegar, cocoa powder and red coloring to impart an unusual, but pleasant flavor. I recommend using a paste coloring as they are more intense and do not affect the cake batter consistency.

Makes: one 23 cm (9 in) round cake or approximately 12 cupcakes

Ingredients

110 g (4 oz) unsalted butter, softened
275 g (10 oz) caster (superfine) sugar
Red paste coloring (enough to turn batter deep red)
90 g (3⅕ oz) egg (room temperature)
275 g (10 oz) cake flour or plain (all purpose) flour
5 g (⅕ oz) bicarbonate of soda
12 g (¼ oz) unsweetened cocoa powder
155 g (5½ oz) sour cream
20 ml (⅔ fl oz) red wine vinegar
700 g (1 lb 5 oz) Cream Cheese Frosting (page 202)

Method

1. You will also need some white chocolate shavings (at least 100 g (3½ oz) and either some ground dried red velvet cake crumbs or some red sugar made by mixing granulated sugar with a little red coloring.

2. Place the butter and sugar into a grease-free plastic bowl and beat together with a wooden spoon until 'light' and 'fluffy' (please refer to the Quality Control Section page 222).

3. Now add the red paste coloring until the batter is deep red.

4. Next the egg is added a bit at a time. Add in at least six separate additions, or many more if you like. If the egg is added too quickly, the batter will curdle. After each addition of egg is incorporated, beat it well before adding the next portion of egg. If you find any signs of water droplets appearing on the batter before all the egg is added, stop adding any more egg and add the flour as described below then add the remaining egg once the flour has been mixed in. By doing this you will retain the batter in the best condition and cause minimal detriment to the potential baked height of the cake.

5. Add the flour, bicarbonate of soda, and cocoa powder to the batter and mix thoroughly to make sure there are no lumps or areas of the batter which have no flour (you can see these as they will be darker in color to that which has the flour incorporated). You can be heavy-handed with this as you are not going to deflate the batter or toughen the cake.

6. Add the sour cream and thoroughly mix into the batter and scrape down the sides of the bowl.

7. Finally add the red wine vinegar and mix thoroughly to achieve a smooth lump-free batter with no areas of different colors (this signifies insufficient mixing or scrapping the sides of the bowl).

8. Line the bottom of the inside of your baking pan with a disc of baking paper and coat the sides in a thin layer of white fat or non-stick spray if you have some.

9. Place the batter in the center of the pan and spread to form an even layer, trying not to get batter up the sides of the pan which will burn.

10. Place the cake pan in your oven on the lower shelf and bake at 170°C (325°F) for 40 minutes or so. This is a little tricky to visually decide if it is baked as it will be red but you should see darkening of the top crust. It will also be springy in the center (Technique 6).

11. When baked, remove the cake pan from your oven, bang the pan and leave in the baking pan to cool down.

12. Remove the red velvet cake from the baking pan and cut in half horizontally (Technique 7).

13. Spread a layer of cream cheese frosting on the cut surface of the bottom half.

14. Place the top back on and cover the top and sides with cream cheese frosting.

15. Press the white chocolate shavings in to the sides of the cake.

16. Sprinkle either red velvet cake crumbs or red colored sugar over the top.

17. This size cake can be cut into 8–10 portions.

Do not combine the sour cream and red wine vinegar together before adding to the batter as it will curdle. Add them separately to the batter, mixing the sour cream through thoroughly before adding the vinegar.

TIP

Place the cake in the fridge once baked and cool. This will firm up the cake and make the cutting in half procedure easier. Never try cutting the cake if frozen.

Passion Cake (gluten-free)

This is a fruitier, slightly tropical version of a carrot cake. When baked it will be a more golden-colored cake, heavier textured and take a longer time to bake in comparison to most other cakes. A simple method to make as you will just stir the ingredients together until thoroughly blended.

Makes: one 23 cm (9 in) round cake

Ingredients

145 g (5 oz) gluten-free self-raising (self-rising) flour
220 g (7¾ oz) caster (superfine) sugar
1.5 g (pinch) mixed spice
1.5 g (pinch) ground ginger
6.5 g (¼ oz) cinnamon
1 g (½ pinch) nutmeg
100 ml (3½ fl oz) vegetable oil
100 g (3½ oz) eggs (room temperature)
250 g (9 oz) grated carrots
80 g (3 oz) tinned pineapple (well drained)
35 g (1¼ oz) desiccated coconut
50 g (1¾ oz) sultanas
40 g (1⅓ oz) pecans (chopped)
350 g (12 oz) Cream Cheese Frosting (make half the recipe on page 202)

Extra desiccated coconut (toasted) is required for sprinkling over the top.

Method

1. Place the gluten-free flour, sugar and spices in a plastic mixing bowl and blend together.
2. Add the oil and eggs and mix into a paste.
3. Add remaining ingredients and mix through thoroughly.
4. Line the bottom of the inside of your baking pan with a disc of baking paper and coat the sides in a thin layer of white fat or non-stick spray if you have some.
5. Place the batter in the center of the pan and spread to form an even layer, trying not to get batter up the sides of the pan, which will burn.
6. Place the pan in your oven on the lower shelf and bake at 170°C (325°F) for 50 minutes or so. It should be golden when baked and springy in the center (Technique 6).
7. When baked, remove from your oven, and leave in the baking pan to cool down.
8. Remove the cake from your baking pan and spread a generous layer of cream cheese frosting over the top.
9. Finally, sprinkle some toasted desiccated coconut over the top.
10. Place in the fridge to firm up before cutting slices (generally 8–10 portions from a 23 cm (9 in) round cake).

Chiffon Cake (enriched sponge)

I would place this in the category of an enriched sponge. The method differs greatly from that of the sugar batter or the Swiss roll sponge. I would say it's a bit like making macarons. You will whisk a meringue and then gently fold that into a paste, trying not to lose the air entrapped in your meringue. The resultant cake will have lightness from the meringue but added tenderness from the vegetable oil.

Makes: one 23 cm (9 in) round cake

Ingredients
280 g (10 oz) Cake (or plain (all purpose) flour)
130 g (4½ oz) caster (superfine) sugar
2 pinches salt
8 g (⅓ oz) baking powder
80 g (3½ oz) egg yolks (room temperature)
80 ml (3½ fl oz) vegetable oil
60 ml (2 fl oz) water (tepid)
160 g (5 oz) egg whites
80 g (3½ oz) caster (superfine) sugar
handful of mixed berries
a pinch of Cream of Tartar (or drop of lemon juice)

You will need to make Swiss Meringue Buttercream for decorating the cake (see page 202).

Method
1. Place the flour, sugar, salt, baking powder into a grease-free plastic bowl and blend together with a wooden spoon.
2. Add the eggs, oil and water and mix until a smooth, lump-free paste is formed.
3. In a separate grease-free bowl whisk the egg whites until light a foam.
4. Add the Cream of Tartar or lemon juice and continue whisking (adding either will strengthen the meringue).
5. Gradually add the sugar, a spoonful at a time, whilst whisking until all the sugar is added. You should be able to turn the bowl upside down without the meringue falling out when ready.
6. You now need to add the meringue into the paste as you would if making macarons (Technique 8).

7. Once incorporated, the batter should be lump-free, a constant color throughout and the consistency should be airy, thick but such that the batter will flow slowly when poured into the baking pan.
8. Place the batter in the center of the pan and spread to form an even layer, trying not to get batter up the sides of the pan, which will burn.
9. Place the cake pan in your oven on the lower shelf and bake at 170°C (325°F) for 35 minutes or so. It should be golden when baked and springy in the center (Technique 6).
10. When baked, remove the cake from your oven, bang the pan and leave in the baking pan to cool down.
11. Remove from baking pan and cut in half horizontally (Technique 7).
12. Spread a layer of Swiss Meringue Buttercream (page 202) on the cut surface of the bottom half.
13. Place on a layer of mixed fresh berries.
14. Place the top back on and cover the top with more buttercream.
15. Randomly scatter mixed berries over the top of the buttercream. The top of the cake should now look fresh and vibrant. This size cake can be cut into 8–10 portions.

TIP

For a children's version of this cake, add lots of colored sugar strands to the paste before adding the meringue. This will create a colorful, speckled appearance when sliced. I would recommend to use the standard buttercream (page 200) for a kids cake, instead of the richer Swiss meringue version.

Guinness Cake

Adding Guinness to a chocolate cake produces a rich pleasant bitterness and works really well with cream cheese frosting, which looks like the 'head' synonymous with a pint of Guinness. This recipe is made in a similar way to a brownie. The baked cake will be more fragile than other cakes in this book so make sure it is chilled before you cut it, to prevent it from crumbling,

Makes: one 23 cm (9 in) round cake

Ingredients

115 g (4 oz) unsalted butter
50 g (1¾ oz) dark Belgian chocolate
250 g (9 oz) caster (superfine) sugar
150 ml (5½ fl oz) Guinness (room temperature)
50 g (1¾ oz) unsweetened cocoa powder
100 g (3½ oz) sour cream
70 g (2½ oz) egg (room temperature)
210 g (7½ oz) cake flour (or plain (all purpose) flour)
7 g (¼ oz) bicarbonate of soda (baking soda)
350 g (12 oz) Cream Cheese Frosting (make half the recipe on page 202)

You will need some grated dark chocolate for sprinkling on top of the frosting (optional).

Method

1. Place the butter and chocolate in a plastic bowl and gently melt in the microwave or over a hot water bath. After it is melted, raise the temperature until it is warm, approximately 50°C (122°F). This will help keep the batter fluid when adding the liquids.
2. In a separate bowl combine the sugar, Guinness and cocoa powder together, and then pour (whilst stirring) into the butter/chocolate mixture.
3. Add the sour cream, mix through and scrape down the sides of the bowl.
4. Add the egg, mix through and scrape down the sides of the bowl.
5. Finally, add the flour and bicarbonate of soda, and then stir until thoroughly combined.

6. Pour the mixture into your baking paper lined 23 cm (9 in) square baking pan. If the batter is still warm it will make its own level. However if the batter has thickened, you will need to spread it level across the baking pan.
7. Place the pan into your oven and bake at 170°C (325°F) for 40 minutes or so. It will be difficult to tell visually when baked but it should feel springy in the center (Technique 6).
8. When baked, remove from your oven, bang the pan and leave in the baking pan to cool down.
9. Remove the baked cake from the baking pan and spread a layer of cream cheese frosting over the top.
10. Scatter some grated dark chocolate over the frosting.

This size cake can be cut into 8–10 portions (but chill it before cutting).

If you prefer to make Guinness Cupcakes then use the recipe above and two-thirds fill your cupcake cakes. You should get approximately twelve cupcakes, depending on the size of your cupcake cases. They will take approximately 25 minutes to bake.

Canadian Coffee Time Cake

This cake reminds me of my visit to a factory in Canada where they were making thousands of these cakes and in many flavor combinations. The cake is made by swirling two different cake batters within large Bundt pans and then it is covered in a crumble topping. This version is vanilla, chocolate and cinnamon. In Canada, this style of cake is very popular.

Makes: one 20 cm (8 in) round Bundt cake

Stage 1——The Cinnamon Crumble

Ingredients
100 g (3½ oz) plain (all purpose) flour
65 g (2⅓ oz) caster (superfine) sugar
2 pinches of cinnamon
40 g (1⅓ oz) unsalted butter, softened

Method
1. Place the flour, sugar and cinnamon in a plastic bowl and mix together.
2. Add the butter and rub through the dry ingredients until a crumble consistency is achieved.

Stage 2–The Cake

Ingredients
185 g (9 oz) unsalted butter, softened
185 g (9 oz) caster (superfine) sugar
185 g (9 oz) egg (room temperature)
185 g (9 oz) self-raising (self-rising) flour
5 g (1/6 oz) unsweetened cocoa powder
5 g (1/6 oz) cinnamon

Method
3. Place the butter and sugar into a grease-free plastic bowl and beat together with a wooden spoon until 'light' and 'fluffy' (please refer to the Quality Control Section page 222).
4. Next the egg is added a bit at a time. Add in at least six separate additions, or many more if you like. If the egg is added too quickly, the batter will curdle. After each addition of egg is incorporated, beat it well before adding the next portion of egg. If you find any signs of water droplets appearing on the batter before all the egg is added, stop adding any more egg and add the flour as described below then add the remaining egg once the flour has been mixed in. By doing this you will retain the batter in the best condition and cause minimal detriment to the potential baked height of the cake.
5. Add the flour to the batter and mix thoroughly to make sure there are no lumps or areas of the batter that have no flour (you can see these as they will be darker in color to that which has the flour incorporated). You can be heavy-handed with this as you are not going to deflate the batter or toughen the cake.
6. Coat the sides and bottom of your Bundt pan in a thin layer of white fat or non-stick spray if you have some.
7. Place 450 g (1 lb) of the batter in the bottom of the pan and spread to form an even layer, trying not to get batter up the sides of the pan which will burn.
8. Add the cocoa powder and cinnamon to the remaining batter and mix through thoroughly.
9. Spoon this batter in dollops into the plain batter already in the baking pan.
10. Using the tip of a knife, swirl the dollops into the plain batter to create a marbled effect.
11. Cover the top of the batter with all of the cinnamon crumble. This will be a thick layer.
12. Using a hand spray containing water, coat the top of the crumble with water (this will help hold the crumble together when you remove the baked cake from the Bundt pan and also when you cut through it).
13. Place the Bundt pan in your oven on the lower shelf

and bake at 180°C (350°F) for 40 minutes or so. It should be golden brown when baked and springy in the center (Technique 6). Some of the cake might pop through the crumble topping.

14. When baked, remove the Bundt pan from your oven, bang the pan and leave in the baking pan to cool down.

15. Gently remove the cake from the Bundt pan trying not to damage the crumble.

16. This size cake can be cut into 8–10 portions.

TIP

Drizzle some toffee sauce over the top of the cake before cutting to add a little extra treat.

Orange Polenta Cake

The addition of polenta to a cake imparts a yellow color, adds a slight flavor and a gritty texture. Some polenta cake recipes do not contain flour and are very dense. My recipe does contain flour and baking powder to help create height and lightness to the cake. The cake is nice to eat soaked in my spicy orange syrup as for a Moroccan style cake.

Makes: one 23 cm (9 in) round cake

Stage 1— Spicy Orange Syrup
Ingredients
Juice of 1 large orange
Juice of 1 lemon
75 g (3 oz) caster (superfine) sugar
2 cloves
1 cinnamon stick

Method
1. Place all the ingredients in a saucepan.
2. Bring to the boil, and then simmer for a few minutes.
3. Remove from heat and leave to cool.
4. Remove the cloves and cinnamon stick before pouring over cake.

Stage 2—For the Cake
Ingredients
250 g (9 oz) unsalted butter, softened
250 g (9 oz) caster (superfine) sugar
250 g (9 oz) egg (room temperature)
125 g (4½ oz) cake flour (or plain (all purpose) flour)
185 g (6½ oz) polenta (fine)
7.5 g (¼ oz) baking powder
Zest of 1 large orange

Method
5. Place the butter and sugar into a grease-free plastic bowl and beat together with a wooden spoon until 'light' and 'fluffy' (page 116).
6. Add in at least six separate additions, or many more if you like. If the egg is added too quickly, the batter will curdle. After each addition of egg is incorporated, beat it well before adding the next portion of egg. If you find any signs of water droplets appearing on the batter before all the egg is added, stop adding any more egg and add the flour as described below then add the remaining egg once the flour has been mixed in. By doing this you will retain the batter in the best condition and cause minimal detriment to the potential baked height of the cake.

7. Add the flour, polenta and baking powder to the batter and mix thoroughly to make sure there are no lumps or areas of the batter which have no dry ingredients (you can see these as they will be a different color to that which has the flour/polenta incorporated). You can be heavy-handed with this as you are not going to deflate the batter or toughen the cake.

8. Line the bottom of the inside of your baking pan with a disc of baking paper and coat the sides in a thin layer of white fat or non-stick spray if you have some.

9. Place the batter in the center of the pan and spread to form an even layer, trying not to get batter up the sides of the pan which will burn.

10. Place the cake pan in your oven on the lower shelf and bake at 170°C (325°F) for 50 minutes or so. It should be golden brown when baked and springy in the center (Technique 6). This cake can collapse in the center if it is moved too early during baking so be very careful with it. It also takes a little longer to set than a Victoria sandwich.

11. When baked, remove from your oven, bang the pan and leave in the baking pan to cool down.

12. To add the syrup, pierce holes through the cake with a skewer.

13. Spoon the syrup over the top, encouraging it to flow into the holes. Let it soak in then add some more until all the syrup has been absorbed.

14. This size cake can be cut into 8–10 portions.

15. The cake eats nicer if you leave it for a day to mature with the syrup, that's if you can wait that long!

Christmas Pudding

Although the quality of mass-produced Christmas Puddings is really good, there is something special about making your own. Yes, it is a long recipe, but it is simple to make and can be prepared months in advance. You can easily purchase the modern plastic lidded pots specific for making Christmas puddings or, if you have the original small basins then use them. You could make a batch, wrap them nicely in cloth, and give them out as Christmas gifts. Baking is carried out in a water bath and reheating can also use this method, or the reheating can be done in the microwave to save a lot of time.

Makes: approximately 1.3 kg (3 lb) of batter

Ingredients

Stage 1
155 g (5½ oz) sultanas
155 g (5½ oz) currants
155 g (5½ oz) Raisins
100 g (3½ oz) mixed peel
zest and juice of 1 lemon
zest and juice of 1 orange
20 ml (⅔ fl oz) rum
20 ml (⅔ fl oz) brandy
20 ml (⅔ fl oz) Grand Marnier
100 g (3½ oz) apple (cooked and sliced)
75 g (2½ oz) egg
30 g (1 oz) black treacle
30 g (1 oz) glycerine

Stage 2
125 g (4½ oz) plain (all purpose) flour
100 g (3½ oz) dark brown sugar
25 g (1 oz) ground almonds
25 g (1 oz) mixed spice
12 g (¼ oz) cinnamon
25 g (1 oz) toasted, flaked almonds
55 g (2 oz) breadcrumbs

Stage 3
125 g (4½ oz) vegetable suet

Method
1. Pre-soak the dried fruits in hot water and drain thoroughly.
2. Place them in a large plastic bowl with the remaining ingredients from stage 1 and mix together.
3. In a separate bowl, place all the ingredients from stage 2 and mix together until thoroughly blended through.
4. Add the powdered ingredients to the fruit mixture and thoroughly combine together.
5. Finally add the vegetable suet and gently mix through (be careful not to damage the suet).
6. Prepare your pots or basins by coating the inside with a light layer of butter.
7. The amount added will vary on the size of your containers but you should aim the three quarters fill them. I place 120 g (4¼ oz) into individual pots and 400 g (14 oz) into a 4 portion size pot.
8. Cover the pots with their lids or foil.
9. Place them into a roasting pan with some water three-quarters up the sides of the pots.
10. Cover the whole roasting pan with foil to keep the steam inside whilst baking.
11. Place the roasting pan into your oven and bake at 140°C (275°F). Time will vary depending on the size of your pot, but as a guide the 120 g (4¼ oz) pots will take 3 hours and the 400 g (14 oz) pots will take 6 hours.

TIPS
* Place a cooling wire rack at the bottom of the water bath for the pots to sit on to protect their bases from over baking.
* If the puddings are kept tightly sealed, they will still be good a year later.

Baked Cheesecake

Voted the most popular dessert in the UK, and it is hard to dispute that. I much prefer this baked cheesecake to the cold-set variety. On its own, it is a lovely heavy and creamy dessert, but it can also be topped in many ways, have a variety of bases and the cheesecake itself can be made into many flavor varieties.

Baked cheesecake is a difficult product to bake, as it is prone to cracking on top. I recommend mastering this plain cheesecake recipe first, before trying out other flavor variants. This way you can establish the best baking technique that works for you in your oven. You will need to bake the cheesecake in a water bath to facilitate gentle heat penetration, which will help to prevent cracking.

Cheesecake can have a sponge or biscuit base. The biscuit base is quicker to make if you use packet biscuits. There are many varieties of biscuits which can be used. If you prefer, you can use your favorite biscuit to replace the digestives used in this recipe.

Makes: one 23 cm (9 in) round cheesecake

Stage 1– Biscuit Base
Ingredients
200 g (7 oz) digestive biscuits
115 g (4 oz) unsalted butter, softened

Method
1. Using a rolling pin break up the biscuits into small pieces.
2. Add the butter to the biscuits and mix together.
3. Place a baking paper disc at the base of your 23 cm (9 in) round loose-bottom cake pan.
4. Pour in the biscuit mix and press down firmly to fill the base level.
5. Wrap the outside bottom and sides of the pan in aluminium foil. This is to prevent water finding its way in the pan when baking in the water bath

Stage 2–Cheesecake Filling
Ingredients
875 g (1 lb 15 oz) cream cheese
300 g (10½ oz) caster (superfine) sugar
15 g (½ oz) cornflour (cornstarch)
9 g (⅓ oz) salt
Few Drops of vanilla extract

130 g (4½ oz) whipping cream
180 g (6½ oz) egg
60 g (2 oz) egg yolk

When combining these ingredients, give the minimal amount of mixing needed to bring the ingredients together.

Method
6. Place the cream cheese in a bowl and mix just until smooth and lump free.
7. In a separate bowl, blend together the sugar, cornflour (cornstarch) and salt. Add this to the cream cheese and slowly blend through. Scrape down the sides of the bowl.
8. Slowly pour in the cream whilst stirring. Scrape down the sides of the bowl.
9. Slowly add the eggs whilst stirring. Scrape down the sides of the bowl and stir again until the cheesecake filling is lump free and smooth.
10. Pour the mixture into your 23 cm (9 in) round pan with the biscuit mix at the base.
11. Place the pan in a roasting tray and fill with water, two-thirds up the sides of the pan.
12. Place the roasting pan into your oven on the lower shelf and bake at 160°C (315°F) for 70–90 minutes. This time will vary depending on your oven. The cheesecake is baked

when the outer rim is firm (and maybe golden brown too) and dull, and the center is still wobbly and glossy.

13. Do not take out the oven. Turn the oven off, leave the door ajar and then leave the oven and the cheesecake to cool down.

14. When at room temperature, remove the cheesecake from the oven and place in your refrigerator for a few hours to firm up. The cheesecake eats so much better after spending at least a few hours in the refrigerator.

TIP

If your cheesecake does crack, don't despair as you can cover the top with fruits, purées or creams to hide it. Only you will know! So why does the cheesecake crack?

There are many theories as to why the cheesecake cracks but I would suggest that the baking and cooling are the main problem areas. The baking must be done gently, and the water bath definitely helps with this. The center portion of the cheesecake must look wobbly and shiny when the baking time is complete, as it will carry on setting for a while longer as it cools. Check the temperature in the center of the cheesecake. If it reaches 65°C (150°F) then it is done. If it gets a little hotter than this temperature, there is a possibility it will crack. If the cheesecake is removed from the oven to cool down, the sudden change in temperature will promote cracking. By placing a baking tray on top of the pan whilst it cools will help to keep the temperature of the cheesecake more even. Alternatively, leave the cheesecake in the oven (switched off) with the door ajar, to cool.

Gluten-Free Orange and Almond Cake

The removal of wheat flour from a cake is necessary to make a gluten-free version, and will change the characteristics of the cake quite significantly. Sole replacement with almonds will produce a frangipane type texture, so I have added some proprietary gluten-free flour blend to re-introduce some 'cakey' texture and improve the baked height. A typical gluten-free flour is a blend of some or all of the following starches; rice, tapioca, potato, maize and buckwheat.

This recipe makes one cake, but it is baked in two separate tins rather than one deep cake cut in half horizontally. After baking, the two halves are soaked in orange syrup and layered with an orange filling. I would recommend using about 500 g (1 lb 2 oz) of either the Buttercream (page 200) or the Swiss Meringue Buttercream (see page 200). Add the zest of one large orange for flavor and a little of the juice if you prefer a softer buttercream.

Recipe Makes: one 23 cm (9in) round cake

Orange Syrup
juice of 1 large orange
75 g (3 oz) caster (superfine) sugar

Method
1. Place all the ingredients in a saucepan.
2. Bring to the boil, and then simmer for a few minutes.
3. Remove from heat and leave to cool.

For the Cake
185 g (6½ oz) softened unsalted nutter
250 g (9 oz) caster (superfine) sugar
250 g (9 oz) egg
125 g (4½ oz) gluten-free plain (all purpose) flour
200 g (7 oz) ground almonds
7.5 g (¼ oz) gluten-free baking powder
zest of 2 large oranges (1 for the cake and 1 for the filling cream)

Method
1. Place the butter and sugar into a grease-free plastic bowl and beat together with a wooden spoon until 'light' and 'fluffy'. (Please refer to the Quality Control Section page 222).
2. Next, half the quantity of the egg is added a bit at a time. Add in at least four separate additions, or many more if you like. If the egg is added too quickly, the batter will curdle. After each addition of egg is incorporated, beat it well before adding the next portion of egg. If you find any signs of water droplets appearing on the batter before all the egg is added, stop adding any more egg and add the gluten-free flour, ground almonds and gluten-free baking powder, as described below, then add the remaining egg once these have been mixed in. By doing this you will retain the batter in the best condition and cause minimal detriment to the potential baked height of the cake.
3. Add the gluten-free flour, ground almonds and gluten-free baking powder to the batter and mix thoroughly to make sure there are no lumps or areas of the batter which have no dry ingredients (you can see these as they will be a different colour to that which has the flour/almonds incorporated). You can be heavy-handed with this, as you are not going to deflate the batter or toughen the cake.
4. Finally add the remaining egg and beat through thoroughly until a smooth and lump-free batter is achieved.
5. Line the bottom of the inside of your baking pans with a disc of baking paper and coat the sides in a thin layer of white fat or non-stick spray if you have some.
6. Place 500 g (1 lb 2 oz) of the batter in the centre of each pan and spread to form an even layer, trying not to get batter up the sides of the pan which will burn.
7. Place both cake pans in your oven on the lower shelf

and bake at 170°C (325°F) for 25 minutes or so. It should be golden brown when baked and lightly springy in the centre (Technique 6). This cake can collapse in the centre if it is moved too early during baking so be very careful with it. When baked, remove from your oven, bang the pan and leave in the baking pan to cool down.

8. To add the syrup, pierce holes through the cake with a skewer.

9. Spoon the syrup over the top, encouraging it to flow into the holes. Let it soak in then add some more until all the syrup has been absorbed.

10. Place the cake in your refrigerator to firm up before finishing.

11. To finish, spread your orange filling on top of one of the cakes then place the other cake on top. Decorate the top with some strips of orange zest or caramelized orange slices.

Note: The cake is nicer if you leave it for a day to mature with the syrup.

This size cake can be cut into 8–10 portions.

Cakes and Sponges

Pastries

I have a refrigerated patisserie counter at Cinnamon Square, and when it is full it looks stunning. Many of the products displayed in this unit are based around sweet pastry. The sweet pastry I make at Cinnamon Square is extremely rich in butter, eggs and ground almonds. This imparts a lovely flavor, a golden color and the perfect shortness when eaten. But the trouble we have with sweet pastry is that the shorter (melt-in-the-mouth) it is, the more fragile and challenging it will be to work with. I have developed a sweet pastry recipe, used in the following chapter, which has wonderful eating qualities whilst still being a workable paste. Be aware though, that if a paste is really easy to roll out without breaking then it will, more than likely, be rock hard to eat once baked!

You will notice that in my recipes you will be using bread flour as part or all of the total flour. This might seem a little unusual, but its incorporation will help to make the paste workable without compromising the eating quality due to the high amounts of butter used.

The method to make the paste is very simple, by firstly blending the powders, then adding the butter (as there is such a lot of butter it will look like a crumbly paste, rather than a crumble at this stage) and finally binding the ingredients to a soft paste with egg. After mixing, the paste will feel soft but it will firm up a little over the following 20 minutes or so. Unless the butter is too soft when added, it should be possible to use the paste immediately. The paste can be refrigerated if too soft, but be careful it is not in there too long otherwise it will become too hard to use.

Any spare paste can be frozen. Make sure it is wrapped tightly in strong plastic. However, as this is a butter pastry it will still go rancid whilst frozen (this could occur after a few months). If you note a cheesy smell after it is defrosted then I would not recommend using the paste.

Also included in this section are my recipe and tips for making perfect choux pastry.

Rich Sweet Pastry

A wonderfully light, sweet pastry rich in butter, eggs and ground almonds. This recipe makes perfect pastry every time!

Makes: Twelve 10 cm (4 in) tartlets

Ingredients

115 g (4 oz) strong bread flour
115 g (4 oz) plain (all purpose) flour
85 g (3 oz) caster (superfine) sugar
85 g (3 oz) ground almonds
170 g (6 oz) unsalted butter, softened (not too soft)
50 g (1¾ oz) egg (cold)

Method

1. Place both flours, sugar and almonds in a plastic bowl and mix them together until thoroughly dispersed.
2. Add the butter and blend with the powders until a smooth paste is formed. Although this will look like a workable paste at this point, it will be crumbly as it still requires the egg to bind it together.
3. Add the egg and gently blend this through. Stop mixing as soon as it comes together.
4. Leave the paste for 20 minutes to firm up a little before use.
5. If it is still too soft to use, then place it in the refrigerator for 20 minutes. Bring it back out and gently knead the paste a little to even out the temperature. Leave it for 5 minutes to firm up. If it is still a bit soft, place it back in the refrigerator for a little longer.

TIP

Replace the ground almonds with roasted ground hazelnuts for a stronger flavored pastry.

Chocolate Sweet Pastry

With the addition of cocoa powder, the pastry is transformed into a chocolately version of the Rich Sweet Pastry. I like to use a dark cocoa powder to impart strong color and flavor.

Makes: approximately twelve 10 cm (4 in) tartlets

Ingredients

210 g (7½ oz) strong bread flour
20 g (⅔ oz) unsweetened cocoa powder
85 g (3 oz) caster (superfine) sugar
85 g (3 oz) ground almonds
170 g (6 oz) unsalted butter, softened (not too soft)
50 g (1¾ oz) egg (cold)

Method

1. Place the bread flour, cocoa powder, sugar and almonds in a plastic bowl and mix them together until thoroughly dispersed.

2. Add the butter and blend with the powders until a smooth paste is formed. Although this will look like a workable paste at this point, it will be crumbly as it still requires the egg to bind it together.

3. Add the egg and gently blend this through. Stop mixing as soon as it comes together.

4. Leave the paste for 20 minutes to firm up a little before use.

5. If it is still too soft to use, then place it in the refrigerator for 20 minutes. Bring it back out and gently knead the paste a little to even out the temperature. Leave it for 5 minutes to firm up. If it is still a bit soft, place it back in the fridge for a little longer.

TIP

When baking chocolate pastry, due to its color it is difficult to judge when it is baked. I recommend you master using and baking the rich sweet pastry recipe in this chapter first, then when it comes to baking the chocolate pastry you know where best to place it in your oven and for how long to bake it for.

Tarte au Citron

A real French classic relies on a high-quality lemon filling to deliver a sharp, pleasant flavor and smooth consistency when eaten. Choose the best non-waxed lemons you can find and you're on to a winner with this recipe. This fresh lemon filling can also be used for layering cakes, filling cupcakes, blending with buttercream or as the center of a lemon meringue pie.

Makes: six 10 cm (4 in) tartlets

Stage 1— Pastry
Ingredients
Use the Rich Sweet Pastry recipe (page 116). This will
  be a little more than you need but you can freeze the
  remainder for next time.

Method
1. Line 6 x 10 cm (4 in) diameter tart cases or you could make a large one around 23 cm (9 in) diameter (Technique 9). Dock the base with a fork to help release any trapped steam during baking.
2. Place the pastry cases on a baking tray and bake at 180°C (350°F) for 15–18 minutes (until golden brown).
3. (Tip 8) If the bottom of your sweet pastry puffs up during baking, press it down with tissue (careful as it will release steam). Do this about 10 minutes into the bake as the pastry will still be flexible and not crack.
4. Remove from your oven and place on a cooling wire rack.

Stage 2— Lemon Filling
Ingredients
200 g (7 oz) unsalted butter, softened
250 g (9 oz) icing (confectioners') sugar
zest and juice of 1 lemon
100 g (3½ oz) egg yolk
50 g (2 oz) egg

Method
1. Firstly, melt the butter in a large saucepan until it turns into a liquid then add the lemon zest, juice and icing (confectioners') sugar. (The sugar with turn lumpy after it has been added to the melted butter. Don't worry, as this will dissolve whilst heating up).
2. Bring this liquid to a boil, stirring to break down the lumps of sugar and to prevent burning at the base of the pan.
3. Mix the egg yolk and whole egg together in a separate large plastic bowl.
4. Carefully, pour the boiled liquid into the eggs, stirring continuously.
5. It might thicken slightly at this point, but will undoubtedly require further heating.
6. Continue to cook the mixture in the pan, stirring continuously to prevent burning), or in the microwave for 30-second increments until it reaches a double cream consistency. There is more chance in burning if placed back on the stovetop to thicken.
7. Pour into baked tart cases just below the top height of the sides, wobble the case a little to level the filling.
8. Set aside to cool.
9. Place a little grated lime and a pistachio nut in center of each tart or dust with icing (confectioners') sugar over a stencil.

TIPS

* To test it has thickened sufficiently before pouring into the art cases, let some filling fall off your spoon in a figure of eight. Rattle the container a little, and if the figure eight nearly disappears then it is ready to pour. It will continue to thicken as it cools (like the baked cheesecake does).
* If you do freeze some of the lemon filling, use it for lemon meringues or as a cake filling once defrosted, as it will be too thick to produce a smooth finish on the Tarte au Citron.

Lemon Meringue Pie

Making lemon meringue pies reminds me of my late Nan who would make one every Saturday when we visited for tea after watching Watford FC play football. Nans always make the best cakes, yet they never weigh anything! How do they do that? I wonder what she would have thought of my measured approach to baking? My Nan's version was baked in the oven to crisp-up the meringue. This version uses an Italian meringue, which after when applied, you will use a blowtorch to brown the outside whilst leaving the inside soft.

Makes: one 30 cm (12 in) pie

Stage 1—Pastry

Method

1. Use the Rich Sweet Pastry recipe on (page 116). This will be a little more than you need but you can freeze the remainder for next time.
2. Line a 30 cm (12 in) diameter flan case (if yours is smaller it is not a problem). (Technique 9). Dock the base with a fork to help release any trapped steam during baking.
3. Place pastry case on a baking tray, Place the pastry cases on a baking tray and bake at 180°C (350°F) for 15–18 minutes (until golden brown).
4. If the bottom of your sweet pastry puffs up during baking, press it down with tissue (careful as it will release steam). Do this about 10 minutes into the bake as the pastry will still be flexible and not crack.
5. Remove from your oven and place on a cooling wire rack.

Stage 2—Lemon Filling

Method

1. Use the filling recipe for Tarte au Citron (page 118)
2. Fill the baked pastry case with a layer of the lemon filling. You can decide the amount you add. I like a nice thick layer.
3. Spread the filling level and leave to cool before adding the Italian meringue.

Stage 3—Italian Meringue Topping

Method

4. Use the Italian meringue recipe (Fillings and Toppings page 189).
5. Once the meringue is made, there are many ways you can apply it to create an attractive appearance.
6. The quickest way, which actually looks really nice, is to cover the filling in the meringue and then use a pallet knife to create a stipple effect by holding the tip of the pallet knife on the surface of the meringue and then lifting it up to create spikes.
7. Sprinkle some flaked almonds over the meringue.
8. Using a blowtorch, carefully brown the top surface of the meringue.
9. Don't hold the blowtorch too close to the meringue otherwise it will burn instantly. The tips of the spikes and the almonds will be the first parts to burn.

Alternatively, using a piping bag with a round, star or rose petal n ozzle you can get really creative in how your meringue is applied. If it all goes wrong, just turn it in to the stippled effect described above.

Raspberry Frangipane

What is frangipane? Well in simple terms it is a heavy, almond-based filling, which is just like making a Victoria Sandwich cake batter but nearly all of the flour is replaced with ground almonds. On its own it would not rise like a cake, and is therefore commonly used in pastry-based tarts as a filling. Many recipes might suggest adding almond extract to boost the flavor. You will note that I do not add this in mine. I prefer the natural flavor achieved from the high level of ground almonds. But feel free to add a few drops if you prefer a more intense flavor.

I recommend part-baking the pastry cases before adding the frangipane mixing to ensure thorough baking of the pastry.

Makes: six 10 cm (4 in) tartlets

Stage 1–Pastry

Method

1. Use the Rich Sweet Pastry recipe (page 116). This will be a little more than you need but you can freeze the remainder for next time.
2. Line six 10 cm (4 in) diameter tart cases (Technique 9). Dock the base with a fork to help release any trapped steam during baking.
3. Place the pastry cases on a baking tray, place into your oven and part bake at 180°C (350°F) for 10–12 minutes (until the top edge just starts to show signs of turning golden).
4. (Tip 8) If the bottom of your sweet pastry puffs up during baking, press it down with tissue (careful as it will release steam). Do this about 10 minutes into the bake as the pastry will still be flexible and not crack. This might be the point you remove them from the oven anyway.
5. Remove from your oven and place on a cooling wire rack.

Stage 2–Frangipane Filling

Ingredients
115 g (4 oz) unsalted butter, softened
115 g (4 oz) caster (superfine) sugar
100 g (3½ oz) egg (room temperature)
115 g (4 oz) ground almonds
20 g (⅔ oz) plain (all purpose) flour

Method

1. Place the butter and sugar into a grease-free plastic bowl and beat together with a wooden spoon until 'light' and 'fluffy' (please refer to the Quality Control Section page 222).
2. Next the egg is added a bit at a time. Add in at least 6 separate additions, or many more if you like. If the egg is added too quickly, the batter will curdle. After each addition of egg is incorporated, beat it well before adding the next portion of egg. If you find any signs of water droplets appearing on the batter before all the egg is added, stop adding any more egg and add the ground almonds and flour then add the remaining egg once the flour has been mixed in. By doing this you will retain the batter in the best condition.
3. Add the almonds and flour to the batter. and mix thoroughly to make sure there are no lumps or areas of the batter which have no almonds or flour (you can see these as they will be darker in color to that which has the almonds and flour incorporated, especially on the sides of the mixing bowl). You can be heavy-handed with this as you are not going to deflate the batter or toughen the frangipane.

Stage 3– Constructing the Raspberry Frangipane

Method

1. Place a layer of frozen (or fresh) raspberries in the part-baked the pastry case.

2. Place the frangipane mixture in a plastic piping bag or use a large strong freezer bag (Tip 7) and fill the pastry case just level to the top edge. If you add too much the frangipane will overflow during baking (you can trim this off after they are baked and cooled, but it will not look as neat).

3. Place the tray of raspberry frangipanes into your oven at 180°C (350°F) for 20–25 minutes (until golden brown in the center).

4. Remove the tray from your oven and place on a cooling wire rack.

5. Spread on a layer of fondant icing. (see page 190)

6. Place a plump raspberry in the center and add a few toasted flaked almonds.

TIPS

* The raspberry on top will bleed into the fondant layer over time, so only place it on top when you are ready to serve or display the finished frangipane.
* Using frozen raspberries underneath the frangipane will help to keep them plump after baking as they spend their first few minutes of the baking process defrosting.

Egg Custard Tarts

A couple of the first sweet products I ever made in the bakery were scones and egg custard tarts. Both are synonymous with British baking. For me, egg custards are best eaten whilst still warm. Traditionally made with milk, I like to substitute some of this with fresh cream to make them a little more luxurious. Freshly ground nutmeg is a must on top.

You can use this egg custard filling recipe to make bread and butter pudding too. For a really modern twist try replacing the bread with sliced croissant, brioche or panettone instead.

Makes: eight 7.5 cm (3 in) tarts

Stage 1—Pastry

Ingredients
Use the Rich Sweet Pastry recipe (page 116). This will be a little more than you need but you can freeze the remainder for next time.

Method
1. Line eight 7.5 cm (3 in) diameter deep pastry cases (Technique 9). Make them a little thicker than you would normally as this will help prevent them from collapsing whilst trying to contain the moist filling.

Stage 2—Egg Custard Filling

Ingredients
350 ml (12 fl oz) milk
150 ml (5½ fl oz) whipping cream
140 g (5 oz) egg
70 g (2½ oz) caster (superfine) sugar

You will also need some freshly ground nutmeg for sprinkling.

Method
1. Place the milk, cream, egg and sugar in a plastic bowl and whisk together.
2. Place your pastry-lined cases on a baking tray and pour in the mixture, filling three-quarters full.
3. Sprinkle some grated nutmeg on top.
4. Carefully place the baking tray into your oven and bake at 180°C (350°F) for 15–20 minutes (until the top of the custard starts to show signs of turning golden). Do not let the custard boil otherwise it will separate. Baking time will vary depending on the depth of your baking pans.
5. When baked, allow to cool on the baking tray.

TIP

Fill the cases as close to your oven as you can. This saves you trying to avoid spilling the custard filling whilst trying to carry the tray.

Fruit Tarts

I like my fruit tarts to have an abundance of fruit and look sensational. Glazing the fruits with a shiny glaze, as simple as an apricot jam, can really enhance their visual appeal, whilst preserving any fruit that has been sliced. Although the fruit is sitting on a bed of crème patissière, I always hide this with the fruit. Unless you are making, for example, strawberry or raspberry fruit tarts, generally they can be a mixture of fruits and it is up to you which ones you use and how you arrange them. Any fruit that is sliced like kiwi, plums and strawberries I would place on the tart first, then immediately glaze before adding other berries or grapes; which do not necessarily require glazing. Pile up some of the fruit to create some height rather than just one flat layer.

Makes: one 30 cm (12 in) pie

You will also require some melted white chocolate and apricot jam for glazing.

Stage 1—Pastry

Method

1. Use the Rich Sweet Pastry recipe (page 116). This will be a little more than you need but you can freeze the remainder for next time.
2. Line a 30 cm (12 in) diameter flan case (if yours is smaller it is not a problem) (Technique 9). Dock the base with a fork to help release any trapped steam during baking.
3. Place the pastry case on a baking tray, Place the pastry cases on a baking tray and bake at 180°C (350°F) for 15–18 minutes (until golden brown).
4. (Tip 8) If the bottom of your sweet pastry puffs up during baking, press it down with tissue (careful as it will release steam). Do this about 10 minutes into the bake as the pastry will still be flexible and not crack.
5. Remove from your oven and place on a cooling wire rack.

Stage 2—Crème Patissière

Method

1. Use the crème patissière recipe (using the 50 per cent extra flour option for a thicker custard—page 203).

2. Once made, cover with plastic wrap and leave to cool down.

Stage 3—Constructing the Fruit Tart

Method

1. Pour the cold crème patissière into the baked pastry case and spread level. You can decide how much filling to add. I prefer a generous amount.
2. Start adding your chosen fruits in the pattern of your choice.
3. Glaze any cut fruits with apricot jam (boiled with a little water to make more fluid), or try using an arrowroot based glaze which imparts a more stable and nicer looking shine.

Once made, consume within three days as it contains crème patissière which has a short shelf life (three days to be safe), plus the fruit will start to look a bit withered by then too.

PAUL'S TOP TIP

Before adding the crème patissière to the baked pastry case, paint the inside of the pastry case with melted white chocolate. This will provide a moisture barrier between the pastry and the crème patissière, thus retaining the crispness of the pastry.

The Orange

Whilst appearing on the television series *Britain's Best Bakery*, we were presented with a brief to make something using shortcrust pastry and orange. We had two weeks to work on it before appearing on the show. Whatever we made had to show innovation and creativity. So rather than coming up with a safe bet, I saw this as a real opportunity to use my passion for product development to enable Cinnamon Square to showcase something special. Thus The orange was born.

Not only was this to contain orange, I wanted it to look like one too.

The orange is made from two halves of orange-colored and flavored sweet pastry. One half is lined in dark chocolate, then filled with an orange and Grand Marnier filling, caramelized oranges (soaked in Grand Marnier), dark chocolate ganache and sealed with a dark chocolate disc. The other half is lined in orange colored and flavored chocolate, filled with an orange mousse and sealed with an orange chocolate disc. The mousse half is then upturned and placed on top of the other half and two leaves are inserted on top as the finishing touch.

It took many hours of development to get the orange to how I had envisaged it as there were many technical challenges to overcome, including how to obtain the actual orange shape. Fortunately, with Cinnamon Square being a coffee shop too, I used small cappuccino cups to bake the orange pastry shells in.

When we finally presented the orange on the television show, the judges were so impressed they claimed it to be the best 'wild card' of the series. A fantastic accolade for those many hours of product development.

The orange is a multi-component product and therefore will take a while to make at home. The stages to make the orange are as follows:
  · Making the orange pastry
  · Lining, freezing, baking and trimming the cappuccino cups with orange pastry
  · Coating the inside of the baked pastry in chocolate
  · Making chocolate discs
  · Caramelising the oranges
  · Making orange and Grand Marnier filling
  · Making dark chocolate ganache
  · Making orange mousse
  · Construction of both halves
  · Inserting the leaves

Makes: 4 oranges (8 halves)

Stage 1— Orange Sweet Pastry

Ingredients

300 g (10½ oz) plain (all purpose) flour
70 g (2½ oz) caster (superfine) sugar
zest of 1 orange
165 g (6 oz) unsalted butter, softened (not too soft)
70 g (2½ oz) egg (cold)
orange paste color

Method

1. Place flour, sugar and orange zest in a plastic bowl and mix them together until nicely dispersed.
2. Add the butter and blend with the powders until a smooth paste is formed. Although this will look like a workable paste at this point, it is actually still crumbly as it still requires the egg to bind it together.
3. Add the egg and some orange paste coloring and gently blend this through. Stop mixing as soon as it comes together.
4. Leave the paste for 20 minutes to firm up a little before use.
5. If it is still too soft to use, then place it in the refrigerator for 20 minutes. Bring back out and gently knead the paste a little to even out the temperature. Leave it for 5 minutes to firm up. If it is still a bit soft, place back in the refrigerator for a little longer.
6. Line eight small cappuccino cups (Technique 9), but leave the paste overhanging the top of the cup to a third down the outside. Press the pastry against the side of the cup to hold in place. Do not grease the cup before adding the paste.
7. Place the pastry-lined cups into your freezer.
8. When fully frozen, place pastry cases on a baking tray, then place the pastry cases on a baking tray and bake at 180°C (350°F) for approximately 15 minutes (the pastry should still look orange). If the orange slips down inside the cup during baking try to press it back up. Be careful as the paste will be very hot.
9. (Tip 8) If the bottom of your sweet pastry puffs up during baking, press it down with tissue (careful as it will release steam). Do this about 10 minutes into the bake as the pastry will still be flexible and not crack.

10. Remove the tray from the oven and leave to cool in the cappuccino cups.
11. When cool, trim the top edge to release the overhanging pastry. You should now be able to remove the remaining pastry shell.
12. Using a guide carefully trim the pastry down to 3 cm (1½in) high with a close serrated tomato paring knife.
13. Paint the inside of four halves with melted dark chocolate and the other four with orange colored and flavored chocolate. It might be difficult to obtain orange chocolate, therefore use dark chocolate for all eight halves.
14. Put aside somewhere safely whilst you work on the other component parts of the orange.

Stage 2——Chocolate Discs

Method

1. Using tempered dark chocolate (tempering method page 206), spread out a thin layer on some thick plastic sheeting (to impart a good shine). Before the chocolate has completely set and by using a circle cutter, press out at least four discs just smaller than the diameter of the pastry shell (at the open end). Always make more than you require to allow for any breakages.
2. Repeat the same with orange-flavored and colored chocolate. Use all dark chocolate if you cannot obtain any orange chocolate.
3. Leave the discs on the plastic until ready to use.

Tip: Use good-quality large freezer bags for the plastic sheeting as they will be thick, sturdy and food grade.

Stage 3— Caramelized Oranges

Method

1. Peel two oranges and place them in a metal pan and drizzle some Grand Marnier on top to soak in.
2. In a separate pan, boil 110 g (4 oz) caster (superfine) sugar with 40 g (1½ oz) water. Leave to boil for a couple of minutes until a light amber color. Pour the sugar syrup over the oranges and leave to soak overnight.

Stage 4– Orange and Grand Marnier Filling

Ingredients
100 g (3½ oz) butter
juice of ½ orange
zest of 1 orange
125 g (4½ oz) icing (confectioners') sugar
70 g (2½ oz) egg yolk
25 g (1 oz) egg
25 ml (1 fl oz) Grand Marnier

Method
1. Firstly, melt the butter in a large saucepan until a liquid then add the orange zest and juice plus the icing (confectioners') sugar. (The sugar with turn lumpy after it has been added to the melted butter. Don't worry, as this will dissolve whilst heating up).
2. Bring this liquid to a boil, stirring to break down the lumps and prevent the bottom of the pan burning.
3. Mix the egg yolk and whole egg together in a separate large plastic bowl.
4. Carefully, pour the boiled liquid into the eggs, stirring continuously.
5. It might thicken slightly at this point, but will undoubtedly require further heating.
6. Continue to cook the mixture back in the pan (stirring continuously to prevent burning) or in the microwave (in 30-second increments until it becomes thick). There is more chance in burning if placed back on the stovetop to thicken. You need this to be thicker than a lemon curd at this point because once the Grand Marnier has been added it will soften to the correct consistency.
7. Add the Grand Marnier and stir through.
8. Cover with plastic wrap and set aside to cool.

Stage 5—Dark Chocolate Ganache

Ingredients
200 g (7 oz) whipping cream
200 g (7 oz) dark chocolate

Method
1. Place the cream in a saucepan and bring to the boil.
2. In a separate bowl, gently melt the chocolate in a microwave, or over a pan of hot water.

3. Pour the melted chocolate into the boiled cream, stirring continuously.
4. Cover and set aside to cool.

Stage 6—Orange Mousse

Only make the mousse when you are ready to start constructing the orange.

Ingredients
5 g (⅕ oz) leaf gelatine
125 ml (4½ fl oz) milk
30 g (1 oz) yolk
40 g (1½ oz) caster (superfine) sugar
juice of ½ orange
zest of 1 orange
65 g (2¼ oz) whipping cream
50 g (1¾ oz) egg whites

Method
1. Soak the leaf gelatine in a little water and set aside.
2. Place the milk in a saucepan and bring to the boil.
3. In a separate bowl blend the egg yolk and sugar together.

4. Add the boiled milk to the egg yolk and sugar mixture and stir through.

5. Place this back into the saucepan and continue heating (and stirring) until it thickens enough to coat the back of a spoon (do not boil as it will separate).

6. Remove the soaked gelatine from the water and place into the custard mixture and stir through until dissolved.

7. Add the orange juice and zest and stir through.

8. Set aside to cool and until it is almost set.

9. In a separate bowl, whisk the cream until fully whipped.

10. In another grease-free bowl whisk the egg whites until it makes soft peaks (add a little Cream of Tartar or lemon juice before it is completely mixed to strengthen the foam).

11. Gently fold the whipped cream into the custard mixture.

12. Finally, gently fold the egg white foam into the mixture trying not to damage the egg whites.

13. Place in the refrigerator until ready to use.

Stage 7—Constructing the Orange—Bottom Half

Method

1. Take four dark-chocolate-lined pastry cases and pipe in some of the orange and Grand Marnier Filling to about a third full.

2. Chop each of the caramelized orange segments into three and place a layer of the cut oranges on top of the orange and Grand Marnier Filling in each pastry case.

3. Using a plastic piping bag or use a large strong freezer bag (Tip 7) pipe the Dark Chocolate Ganache over the oranges to just below the level of the top edge of the pastry to allow room for the chocolate disc to fit in. If the ganache is too firm to pipe, warm it gently in the microwave on medium for 10 seconds at a time.

4. Place on the Dark Chocolate Disc so it is level with the top edge of the pastry—do not place the chocolate disc on if the ganache is warm from softening, as it will melt the chocolate disc.

5. Finally seal the gap between the chocolate disc and pastry with some melted chocolate. Use a small piping bag with a tiny hole cut out.

6. Place the 4 orange bases in the fridge to set the chocolate.

Stage 8—Constructing the orange—Top Half

Method

1. Using the remaining four chocolate-lined pastry cases lined with orange chocolate (or dark chocolate if none available), fill them just below the top edge of the pastry cases with the orange Mousse while leaving room for the chocolate disc.

2. Place on the orange Chocolate Disc (or Dark Chocolate Disc if no orange is available) onto the mousse layer so that it is level with the top edge of the pastry.

3. Finally seal the gap between the chocolate disc and pastry with some melted chocolate. Use a small piping bag with a tiny hole cut out.

4. Place the four orange tops in the fridge to set the chocolate.

5. When set, remove from the fridge and turn over onto a piece of baking paper to keep the chocolate surface clean.

6. Using a skewer, carefully pierce a hole through the pastry in the center at the top of the half dome.

7. Insert the stems of two sugar leaves or even real orange leaves into pastry.

8. Now place this on top of one of the bottom halves and then repeat with the other three sets.

9. You should now have four stunning pastry oranges. Store them in the refrigerator. They should last up to five days (if not already eaten by then!)

If you could not obtain any orange-colored and flavored chocolate and therefore used dark chocolate on the top half as well as the bottom, they will all look the same. Fortunately, the bottom half will feel heavier than the top half (if they get muddled up).

Tarte au Chocolat

The whole experience of eating a chocolate tart is governed by the quality of the chocolate used in the ganache. I only use Belcolade Belgium chocolate in my baking, but then again I did work for them, so I have a 'soft spot' for their chocolate. Just make sure the chocolate you purchase is top quality and that you do not use the cheaper imitation chocolate.

Makes: six 10 cm (4 in) tartlets

Stage 1—Pastry
Use the Chocolate Sweet Pastry recipe on (page 117). This will be a little more than you need but you can freeze the remainder for next time.

Method
1. Line six 10 cm (4 in) diameter tart cases (Technique 9). Dock the base with a fork to help release any trapped steam during baking.
2. Place the pastry cases on a baking tray, Place the pastry cases on a baking tray and bake at 180°C (350°F) for 15–18 minutes (until golden brown).
3. This will be harder to judge but you will see the pastry start to darken.
4. If the bottom of your sweet pastry puffs up during baking, press it down with tissue (careful as it will release steam). Do this about 10 minutes into the bake as the pastry will still be flexible and not crack.
5. Remove the pastry cases from your oven and place on a cooling wire rack.

Stage 2—Dark Chocolate Ganache Filling
Ingredients
400 g (14 oz) whipping cream
400 g (14 oz) dark chocolate
120 ml (4¼ fl oz) glucose syrup (optional)

Method
1. Place the cream in a saucepan and bring to the boil.
2. Add the glucose to the boiled cream.
3. In a separate bowl, gently melt the chocolate in a microwave, or over a pan of hot water.

4. Pour the melted chocolate into the boiled cream, stirring continuously.
5. This will make a little more ganache than you require. You can store the remainder in the refrigerator for at least a couple of weeks.

> Glucose Syrup is added to impart extra shine to the ganache. If you cannot obtain any, then you can remove this from the recipe without other changes.

Stage 3—Construction of the Tarte au Chocolat
Method
1. Remove the baked chocolate pastry cases from their containers.
2. Slowly pour the ganache into each of the baked chocolate pastry cases filling up just short of the top edge.
3. Set aside to cool and set at room temperature. This will take a few hours. Do not move them during this period as they will wrinkle on top.
4. Once completely set, place and store in the refrigerator. The tops can be left undecorated, or you can dust them with cocoa powder through a stencil, which looks really nice against the glossy ganache. Alternatively you can grate some chocolate on top or place on a white chocolate stick.

TIP

If you have some air bubbles on the surface of the ganache, pop with the tip of a knife or a pin. Do this immediately once poured; whist the ganache is still fluid.

Mince Pies (GTA)

TIP

You can make the mincemeat months in advance, as it keeps really well and it also matures too.

I must confess to being a mince pie addict. However, I resist the temptation of making them all year round and settle for making them only over the Christmas period. This recipe is based on my Great Taste Gold Award-Winning mince pie and I do hope you enjoy it, as I do. I make a fairly large individual mince pie at Cinnamon Square but you could make whatever size you would normally choose. I place a pastry star on top leaving some of the mincemeat exposed, but it can be completely covered if you wish.

Makes: six 10 cm (4 in) tartlets

Stage 1—Pastry
Method
1. Use the Rich Sweet Pastry recipe (page 116).
2. Line six 10 cm (4 in) diameter tart cases (Technique 9). Dock the base with a fork to help release any trapped steam during baking.
3. Place the pastry cases on a baking tray, then place in your oven and part bake at 180°C (350°F) for 10–12 minutes (until the top edge just starts to show signs of turning golden).
4. (Tip 8) If the bottom of your sweet pastry puffs up during baking, press it down with tissue (careful as it will release steam). Do this about 10 minutes into the bake as the pastry will still be flexible and not crack. This might be the point at which you remove them from the oven anyway.
5. Using more of the pastry, roll out some as above and cut out some star shapes. The size needs to be large enough to fit close to the inside edge of your pastry cases.
6. Carefully place stars on a baking tray, then place in your oven and part bake at 180°C (350°F) for 8–10 minutes (try not to have any coloring of the paste).

Stage 2—Mincemeat Filling
Ingredients
125 g (4½ oz) sultanas
125 g (4½ oz) currants
50 g (1¾ oz) mixed peel
125 g (4½ oz) raw (demerara) sugar
15 g (½ oz) toasted flaked almonds
7 g (¼ oz) mixed spice
7 g (¼ oz) cinnamon
7 g (¼ oz) nutmeg
185 g (6½ oz) apple pie filling
juice and zest of ½ orange
juice and zestof ½ lemon
15 ml (½ fl oz) rum
15 ml (½ fl oz) brandy
60 g (2 oz) unsalted butter, melted
125 g (4½ oz) vegetable suet

Method
1. Place all the ingredients (except for melted butter and suet) in a large plastic bowl and stir together until thoroughly mixed.
2. Gently melt the butter in the microwave or over a pan of hot water and then stir through the fruit mixture.
3. Finally, add the suet to the mixture and gently fold through until evenly dispersed.
4. Be careful not to damage the suet pieces as you fold them through the mixture.

Stage 3—Mince Pie Construction
Method
5. Place 85 g (3 oz) of the mincemeat filling into the part bake the pastry cake and flatten level.
6. Place a partly baked pastry star on top of the filling.
7. Spray a little water over the top of the pastry and sprinkle with raw sugar.
8. Place the filled pastry cases onto a baking tray, then Place the pastry cases on a baking tray and bake at 180°C (350°F) for 12–15 minutes (until golden brown). If you intend to reheat the baked mince pies to serve them warm the following day for example, then I recommend not bake them too much (light golden brown). Reheating will generally take approximately 5 minutes at 180°C (350°F) and be careful because you can quickly over bake.

Pecan Pie

I like my pecan pie warm with a large dollop of ice cream. At Cinnamon Square we only make this in the cold autumn and winter months and it makes a great thanksgiving dessert. This recipe is for a large pie and requires the pastry to be part baked before being filled with the pecan filling.

Makes: one 30 cm (12 in) Pie

Stage 1—Pastry

Method

1. Use the Rich Sweet Pastry recipe on page 116. This will be a little more than you need but you can freeze the remainder for next time.

2. Line a 30 cm (12 in) diameter flan case (Technique 9). Dock the base with a fork to help release any trapped steam during baking.

3. Place the pastry case on a baking tray, then Place the pastry cases on a baking tray and bake at 180°C (350°F) for 10–12 minutes (try not to have any coloring of the paste).

4. If the bottom of your sweet pastry puffs up during baking, press it down with tissue (careful as it will release steam). Do this about 10 minutes into the bake as the pastry will still be flexible and not crack (this could be when you take the pastry case out anyway).

5. Remove from your oven and place on a cooling wire rack.

Stage 2—Pecan Filling

Ingredients

55 g (2 oz) caster (superfine) sugar
55 g (2 oz) raw (demerara) sugar
80 ml (3 fl oz) golden syrup (or maple syrup)
170 g (6 oz) egg
55 g (2 oz) unsalted butter, melted
170 g (6 oz) pecans, roughly chopped
You will require extra whole pecans for decoration

Method

1. In a plastic bowl, place the sugars, syrup and egg, and then mix together.

2. In a separate bowl, carefully melt the butter either in the microwave or over a pan of hot water.

3. Add the melted butter to the mixture and stir through thoroughly.

4. Finally add the pecans and stir through thoroughly.

5. Make sure the pastry case is still on a baking tray and then pour the mixture into it, so it is filled to just under the top edge of the crust (if you do this close to the oven you will not have too far to carry it, whilst trying not to spill it).

6. Place some whole pecans on the top for decoration.

7. Very carefully, place the tray into your oven and bake at 180°C (350°F) for 25–30 minutes (until the middle feels set).

8. Remove from your oven and leave on the baking tray to cool.

TIP

Replace the ground almonds in the pastry with ground pecans. You will have to make this yourself by grinding the pecans in a food processor.

Linzer Torte

The Linzer Torte is said to be one of the oldest confections—dating back to the 1600s—originating from Austria and named after the city of Linz. A rich and flavorsome pastry encases a blackcurrant preserve and it traditionally has a lattice top made from the same pastry. A winner with me as blackcurrant is my favorite fruit, but you can replace this with your own favorite fruit preserve if you prefer.

Makes: one 25 cm (10 in) Torte

Ingredients

115 g (4 oz) strong bread flour
115 g (4 oz) plain (all purpose) flour
85 g (3 oz) caster (superfine) sugar
85 g (3 oz) roasted ground hazelnuts
15 g (½ oz) ground cinnamon
small pinch ground clove
170 g (6 oz) unsalted butter, softened (not too soft)
50 g (1¾ oz) egg (cold)
You will also need a 340 g (12 oz) jar of blackcurrant
    preserve (top quality).

Method

1. To roast and grind the hazelnuts (optional) you can use packet ground hazelnuts, although these are not as easy to acquire as ground almonds. Alternatively, you can make your own by placing whole hazelnuts on a baking sheet and bake at 180°C (350°F) for approximately 15 minutes until they are fragrant and the outer skins begin to flake and crack. Remove the baking sheet from your oven and leave to cool. Once cooled, remove any skin from the hazelnuts and discard. Place 85 g (3 oz) of the hazelnuts plus 50 g (1¾ oz) of plain (all purpose) flour (leaving 65 g (2⅓ oz) in the recipe above), and blend until finely ground. The addition of a little flour helps prevent the hazelnuts from becoming too oily whilst in the food processor.

Stage 1—Pastry
Method

1. Place both flours, sugar, ground hazelnuts, cinnamon and clove in a plastic bowl and mix them together until thoroughly dispersed.

2. Add the butter and blend through the powders until a smooth paste is formed. Although this will look like a workable paste at this point, it will be crumbly as it still requires the egg to bind it together.

3. Add the egg and gently blend this through. Stop mixing as soon as it comes together.

4. Leave the paste for 20 minutes to firm up a little before use.

5. If it is still too soft to use, then place it in the refrigerator for 20 minutes. Bring it back out and gently knead the paste a little to even out the temperature. Leave it for 5 minutes to firm up. If it is still a bit soft, place back in the fridge for a little longer.

Stage 2—Construction of the Linzer Torte

Method

1. Line a 25 cm (10 in) diameter flan case with low sides, (Technique 9) using the Linzer pastry.

2. Spread on a generous layer of blackcurrant preserve.

3. Now roll the remaining pastry and cut strips (using a pizza wheel) of 2.5 cm (1 in) thick to make the lattice top.

4. Place the strips of pastry on a baking paper lined baking sheet and place in the refrigerator for about 10 minutes.

5. When strips are firm, using a pallet knife, gently transfer the strips to the pastry case (when the strips are cold they are not pliable, but after a minute they will be soft enough to bend). Lay half the strips, evenly spaced, across the top of the torte, rotate the pan 90 degrees and lay the remaining strips across the first strips. Alternatively, weave the top strips over and under the bottom strips (a bit more tricky and more liable to break). Trim the ends of the strips to form a neat edge. You could also make a rope with any remaining pastry and place around the edge and use marzipan pinchers to create a pattern for extra decoration (optional).

6. Place your Linzer torte on a baking tray and bake at 180°C (350°F) for approximately 30 minutes.

7. Remove from your oven, place on a cooling wire rack and leave until cold before cutting.

Choux Pastry—Profiterole Tower

The method to make choux pastry is similar to that of a roux; by boiling milk and butter then cooking in some flour, but then egg is added to turn it into a pipeable paste. In the oven, the paste erupts and expands into a hollow ball, which requires drying out, otherwise the center remains wet and doughy. The amount of egg added will vary depending on how much cooking the flour receives. This is a critical part of the process because the amount of egg added will govern the batter consistency. If the batter consistency is not correct, the choux pastry will not expand perfectly. Therefore, although there is a precise amount of egg detailed in the recipe, you might actually use slightly more, or less, to achieve the correct batter consistency.

To build the profiterole tower you will also need to make crème patissière to fill the choux pastry balls and milk chocolate ganache to dip them in. If you prefer, you could use whipped cream instead of crème patissière to fill them. These balls will be much lighter using whipped cream.

Makes: approximately 30 profiteroles

Ingredients
100 g (3½ oz) butter
200 ml (7 fl oz) water
125 ml (4½ fl oz) milk
150 g (5½ oz) plain (all purpose) flour
180 g (6½ oz) egg (+/−)

Stage 1—Pastry

Method
1. Place the butter, water and milk in a deep saucepan and bring to the boil.
2. Take off the heat and add the flour, mixing continuously with a wooden spoon to remove the lumps.
3. Place back on a medium heat and 'cook' the flour for 1 minute, stirring continuously (this should come together as a ball of paste with the paste not sticking to the edges of the saucepan).
4. Remove from the heat and allow to cool, using a mixer with a beater attachment or by stirring randomly with a wooden spoon.
5. When cool, start adding the egg in small additions, beating well between each addition.
6. Stop adding the egg when the batter takes on 'silky' sheen and makes a 'V' shape when hanging off the end of a spatula.
7. Place the choux paste in a piping bag with a round nozzle and pipe bulbs (Technique 10) approximately 3.5 cm (1½ in) diameter onto a baking tray lined with baking paper (you might require two trays).
8. Bake at 200°C (400°F) for 25–30 minutes until golden all over. If the sides are a creamy white color and the tops golden, they are not fully baked. They will collapse back during cooling and the inside will still be wet.
9. When baked, remove the tray from your oven and leave to cool on the baking tray.

TIP

To help dry the insides of profiteroles out, turn down the oven to 180°C (350°F) after about 20 minutes and lay a sheet of baking paper over the top of the profiteroles. Give them another 10 minutes or more, until they feel crispy and hollow and the sides are golden.

Stage 2—Crème Patissière

Method

1. Use the Crème Patissière recipe on (page 203)
2. Once made, cover with plastic wrap and leave to cool down.

Stage 3—Milk Chocolate Ganache

Ingredients
250 ml (9 fl oz) fresh whipping cream
375 g (13 oz) milk chocolate

Method

1. Place the cream in a saucepan and bring to the boil.
2. In a separate bowl, gently melt the chocolate in a microwave, or over a pan of hot water.
3. Pour the melted chocolate into the boiled cream, stirring continuously.
4. Cover and set aside to cool and start setting.
5. The ideal consistency for dipping the profiteroles into is soft to touch but it will not flow if the container if tipped slightly. Try dipping a ball into the ganache, it needs to coat it and stay in situ, without flowing down to the base.

Stage 4—Profiterole Tower Construction

Method

1. Using the tip of a pair of scissors, pierce a hole in the base of each profiterole (this is where you will pipe in the Crème Patissière.
2. Using a plastic piping bag or use a large strong freezer bag (Tip 7) pipe the Crème Patissière into each of the profiteroles and scrape off any excess which protrudes out of the hole. Place the balls, hole side down, onto some baking paper.
3. When the ganache is at the correct consistency you can now start dipping the tops of the filled balls and placing them on a cake board or plate. You will need to work out how many balls you have on each layer depending on how many balls you ended up with. At least a third of them will make up the base layer.
4. You could construct this tower in one go, or depending on how stable the balls are, you might need to refrigerate between each layer to set the ganache, making the tower

more robust to take the weight of the next layer.
5. When the tower is built you can leave as is, grate some chocolate over it, dust a little cocoa powder or even sprinkle some gold stars/glitter to give it a bit of bling.
6. Keep it stored in the fridge until required.

PAUL'S TOP TIP

Freeze the filled balls for an hour before dipping. This will firm up the balls, making them more robust when being dipped in the ganache. As this makes the balls colder, it also helps to set the ganache (if a little soft). Piling them up to make the tower is easier too as they do not squash so readily.

Jam Roly Poly

I do like a stodgy pudding and this is my favorite, probably as it brings back memories of my childhood treats. It is a pastry but uses suet as the fat. It is very quick to prepare the Roly Poly ready for baking, and once out of the oven it is best eaten straight away as it does not keep well. If left to cool and reheated it will be tough. In my opinion it has to be eaten with thick custard, so make some whilst it is baking.

Makes: enough for 4 people to share

Ingredients

300 g (10½ oz) self-raising (self-rising) flour
85 g (3 oz) caster (superfine) sugar
140 g (5 oz) vegetable suet
175 ml (6 fl oz) cold milk
200 g (7 oz) raspberry jam (or your preferred jam alternative)

You will need a little extra milk and caster (superfine) sugar for decoration.

Method

1. Place the flour, sugar and suet in a plastic bowl and mix together.
2. Add the milk and stir to bring together to a dough (try not to damage the suet).
3. Turn out the dough onto the table and knead a little to bring the dough nicely together.
4. Using plenty of flour to stop the dough form sticking, roll out the dough to a rectangle measuring 20 cm (8 in) high x 30 cm (12 in) wide.
5. Spread the jam over the surface but leave 5 cm (2 in) gap around the edges.
6. Paint the un-jammed edges with a little milk.
7. Starting from the edge furthest away, fold it over and gently roll it up as for a Swiss roll. Try not to push your finger through the dough.
8. Place on a baking tray lined with baking paper with the seam edge underneath and fold the two opposite ends underneath to seal in the jam.
9. Lightly brush any flour off the outer surface and then paint the top with milk. Try not to get any milk on the paper as this will burn the base of your Roly Poly.
10. Generously sprinkle the top surface with caster (superfine) sugar.
11. Place the tray into your oven and bake at 200°C (400°F) for approximately 35 minutes—until you get a nice golden color and there might be some jam bursting through.
12. Remove the baked Roly Poly from your oven and allow to stand for 5 minutes before cutting slices and serving with some thick custard. Beware; the jam will be boiling when the tray is removed from your oven.

TIP

Roly Poly is best served immediately from the oven, as it toughens up the next day. If using this as a dessert, I recommend preparing it ready to bake, then store it in the refrigerator until required.

Laminated Pastries

In this section I have selected recipes based on Puff Pastry and Danish Pastry. Both have one thing in common, they require a dough which has a large quantity of butter encased within it, which is then rolled out and folded to create many layers of dough and butter. When either pastry type is baked, steam is released from the dough and is trapped underneath the butter layers, creating lift and separation. Apart from that, puff pastry and Danish pastry are very different in many ways.

Puff pastry dough is very basic and unyeasted. After the dough is formed, the butter is encased and then it is rolled out, folded into three. It is rolled out and folded a total of six times before it is finally processed into products like Eccles Cakes, Millefoglie or gâteaux Pithivier.

Danish Pastry dough differs greatly as, not only is it enriched, but it also contains yeast. Like puff pastry, it has butter encased in it and it is processed in the same way but only rolled and folded a total of three times before making the desired shapes.

When it comes to baking, puff pastry relies solely on the steam entrapment creating pressure underneath the butter layers to create lift. Whereas in a Danish pastry dough, although the steam entrapment still occurs, there is also the yeast producing carbon dioxide gas which will also create expansion in the dough layers.

As puff pastry is unyeasted, it freezes well in its unbaked state. Therefore most home bakers–and even craft bakeries–will buy in ready-to-roll pastry as it is readily available in supermarkets. However, as Danish pastry is yeasted, it does not keep so well in the freezer and therefore it is commonplace to make it from scratch.

You will notice that in the recipes the total flour content is a combination of both bread and plain (all purpose) flours. This is important because we need the dough to be elastic and strong enough to hold together but also extensible to allow for the constant stretching and folding action during lamination. By replacing some bread flour with plain (all purpose) flour it allows the dough to be stretched more easily, but retain enough strength to make great-looking pastries.

To make the best tasting, laminated pastries you need to use butter. The problem with butter is that it turns from being rock hard to oil very quickly when using it, therefore not only is the temperature of your ingredients important, but so is that of the room you make it in. If the butter used is too hard, it will fracture during the rolling and folding, as it not malleable. If, however, it is too soft it will run out of the dough and make processing extremely difficult and worst case; impossible. I run a Croissant and Danish Pastries Masterclass at Cinnamon Square but only in the autumn and winter, due to the room temperature being too unpredictable in the warmer months.

Croissants

A classic breakfast pastry found in most countries nowadays. Croissants are made from a yeasted enriched dough, which is laminated with butter to create a light and flaky pastry. The shape is created from rolling up triangles of the laminated croissant dough.

Makes: 10 Croissants

Ingredients
300 g (10½ oz) white bread flour
300 g (10½ oz) plain (all purpose) flour
10 g (¼ oz) salt
30 g (1 oz) caster (superfine) sugar
30 g (1 oz) fresh yeast OR 15 g (⅛ oz) dried yeast
15 g (½ oz) unsalted butter, softened
200 ml (7 fl oz) milk (cold)
120 ml (4 ¼ fl oz) water (cold)
270 g (9½ oz) unsalted butter for laminating (good quality)

Method
1. Firstly, prepare the laminating butter by rolling it out to 20 cm (8 in) high x 25 cm (10 in) wide, using plenty of flour to prevent sticking or place between two sheets of baking paper. Keep in the fridge until ready to use.
2. Weigh all the dry ingredients separately, then place them in a plastic bowl, flour first then the rest in separate piles on top including the butter.
3. Add the milk and water, and then combine together until a dough starts to form and the sides of the bowl are clean.
4. Remove the dough from the bowl and knead (Technique 1) on your work surface until it becomes smooth and elastic (approximately 10–12 minutes). This dough does not need to be as fully developed as for a typical bread dough, as it will receive further development whilst it is being rolled and folded.
5. Form the dough into a sausage shape and place in a lidded plastic box and leave to rest for 10 minutes.
6. Remove the dough from the plastic box and, using a rolling pin, roll out the dough into a rectangle measuring 25 cm (10 in) high x 45 cm (18 in) wide.
7. Place the prepared and cold (but malleable) laminating butter over two-thirds of the dough. Fold into three starting with the surface that has no butter on—making sure the dough and butter layers are separated and no butter is protruding out of the sides.
8. This butter is now incorporated into the dough and three half turns are required.
9. Each half turn means rolling dough to 25 cm (10 in) high x 45 cm (18 in) wide, then folding into three and leaving it to rest for 5–10 minutes. Do this three times and then place back in your lidded plastic box and leave for 20 minutes to rest (in the refrigerator if the butter is very soft or leaking out of the dough).
10. Remove the pastry from the plastic box and gently roll out to 38 cm (15 in) high x 42 cm (17 in) wide. If you take your time doing this, you will reduce the chances of the butter coming through the dough onto the outer surface, which will make the rest of the process sticky and very difficult to manage, also affecting the finished pastries.
11. Using a pizza roller cutter, trim off the outer edge to neaten the rectangle to 36 cm (14 in) high x 40 cm (16 in) wide. Cut this in half to make two strips of 36 cm (14 in) wide x 20 cm (8 in) high. You should now have two identically-sized halves.
12. Place one of the strips in front of you in landscape orientation. At the top edge, measure and mark every 12 cm (just under 5 in). You should have two marks. Do the same with the bottom edge but mark the first point at 6 cm (just over 2 in) in from the corner, then the next two 12 cm (just under 5 in) on from the first point.
13. Now cut (use the pizza wheel) the pastry from the top left corner down to the bottom mark which was 6 cm (just over 2 in) in from the bottom corner. Now cut from

the bottom to the first mark at the top to create the first triangle. From the same point at the top cut downwards to the second mark at the base and this will create another triangle. Keep cutting at angles to end up with five triangles and two pieces of scrap at the ends.

14. Repeat this with the second half of pastry to end up with 10 triangles measuring 20 cm (8 in) long x 12 cm (just under 5 in) wide.

15. Starting from the wide end, roll up the pastry into a croissant. If you gently stretch the dough at the pointed end whilst rolling up like a Swiss roll you can increase the number of rotations in the croissant.

16. They can be left straight or shaped into a crescent.

17. Place them onto a baking tray lined with baking paper and brush the tops with some beaten egg (trying not to get it on the tray as it will burn). Allow room for the croissants to expand during both proving and baking.

18. Place the tray in your lidded plastic box to prove for 30-40 minutes. There will be much more expansion in the oven as they bake, than what they will achieve whilst proving.

19. Bake at 200°C (400°F) until golden brown (approximately 20 minutes).

20. Remove the tray from your oven and place the croissants directly on a cooling wire rack to help retain the crispiness of the pastry.

For an extra treat, when they are cool, slice a croissant in half horizontally and spread a generous layer of milk chocolate ganache inside. Place the top back on and dust liberally with icing (confectioners') sugar.

TIP

You will end up with off cuts of pastry with this recipe. I recommend you make some Monkey Bread (see page 158) by cutting strips 1 cm (½ in) wide and 2.5 cm (1 in) long (they do not need to be exact), and then dipping the strips in melted butter and rolling in cinnamon sugar.

Pain au Chocolat

For the Pain au Chocolat we will use the same dough as for the croissants. In the bakery trade we can purchase chocolate strips ready for using inside called croissant bars. If you can source these, they are perfect. If not, then you could use some dark chocolate drops (suitable for baking) and line them up as a strip of chocolate, as you will note in the final stages of this recipe.

Makes: 12 Pain au Chocolate

Ingredients
See Croissants recipe (page 148) for ingredients.

Method

1. Use the recipe and method as used for the Croissants (page 148) until you have left the fully-laminated dough to relax for 20 minutes (in the refrigerator if the butter is very soft or leaking out of the dough).

2. Remove the pastry from the plastic box and gently roll out to 45 cm (18 in) high x 34 cm (14 in) wide. If you take your time doing this, you will reduce the chances of the butter coming through the dough onto the outer surface, which will make the rest of the process sticky and very difficult to manage, also affecting the finished pastries.

3. Using a pizza roller cutter, trim off the outer edge to neaten the rectangle to 44 cm (17 in) high x 33 cm (13½ in) wide.

4. Cut strips measuring 11 cm (4½ in) high x 33 cm (13 in) wide. You should now have four identically-sized strips.

5. Place one of the strips in front of you in landscape orientation. At the top edge, measure and mark every 11 cm (just under 4½ in). You should have two marks. Do the same with the bottom edge.

6. Cut out (using the pizza wheel) three equal squares.

7. Repeat this with the other three pastry strips to end up with 12 pieces of pastry measuring 11 cm (just under 4½ in) squared.

8. Place two croissant bars (or a line of bakeable dark-chocolate chips approximately 2 cm (1 in) inwards from the opposite edges.

9. Brush a little water down the center and fold both edges over the chocolate into the middle and press to secure.

10. Turn this pastry over so that the seam is now underneath.

11. Place them onto a baking tray lined with baking paper and brush the tops with some beaten egg (trying not to get it on the tray as it will burn). Allow room for the Pan au Chocolate to expand during both proving and baking.

12. Place tray in your lidded plastic box to prove for 30–40 minutes. There will be much more expansion in the oven as they bake, than what they will achieve whilst proving.

13. Place the tray into your oven and bake at 200°C (400°F) until golden brown (approximately 15–18 minutes).

14. Remove from oven and place on a cooling wire rack to help retain the crispiness of the pastry.

> **TIP**
>
> You will end up with offcuts of pastry with this recipe. I recommend you make some Monkey Bread (see page 158) by cutting strips 1 cm (½ in) wide and 2.5 cm (1 in) long (they do not need to be exact), dipping in melted butter and rolling in cinnamon sugar.

Lardy Cake

A classic bakery product from yesteryear, containing out of fashion lard. I remember staying with my Grandfather in Brightlingsea during my school summer holidays and every Saturday morning we would walk to local the bakery to buy his favorite lardy cake. It is a fruited bun dough with lard laminated in to it. Lard is the tradition, and after all, it is named after the fat. But if lard is not for you, then replace it with butter. You will require a 25 cm (10 in) round cake pan to bake it in.

Makes: 1 large Lardy Cake—9 portions

Stage 1— Lardy Cake Laminating Filling
Ingredients
60 g (2 oz) caster (superfine) sugar
60 g (2 oz) Lard

Method
1. Combine both ingredients in a bowl with a spoon until thoroughly mixed together.

Stage 2—Dough
Ingredients
310 g (11 oz) strong white bread flour
3 g (pinch and a half) salt
35 g (1⅕ oz) caster (superfine) sugar
20 g (⅔ oz) fresh yeast OR 10 g (¼ oz) of dried yeast
35 g (1⅕ oz) butter (unsalted and softened)
24 g (1 oz) egg (room temperature)
55 ml (2 fl oz) water (tepid)
90 ml (3⅕ fl oz) semi-skimmed milk (lukewarm)
100 g (3½ oz) currants (pre-soaked and drained)
50 g (1¾ oz) sultanas (pre-soaked and drained)

Method
1. Weigh all the dry ingredients separately, then place them in a plastic bowl, flour first then the rest in separate piles on top including the unsalted butter, softened.
2. Add the egg, water and milk, and then combine together until a dough starts to form and the sides of the bowl are clean.
3. Remove the dough from the bowl and knead (Technique 1) on your work surface until it becomes smooth and elastic (approximately 12–15 minutes). Expect the dough to feel soft and sticky for the first few minutes of the kneading process.

4. Use the windowpane test (Technique 3) to check if the dough is fully developed.
5. Form the dough into a sausage/cylinder shape and place in a lidded plastic box and leave to bulk ferment (Fact 1) for 50 minutes.
6. Remove the fermented dough from box and, using a rolling pin, roll the dough to a rectangle 22 cm (9 in) high x 33 cm (13½ in) wide.
7. Position the dough with the 22 cm (9 in) edge closest to you.
8. Using a pallet knife, spread the lardy cake filling over two-thirds of the dough (from left to right).
9. Fold into three by folding the side with no filling on over first, then the side with filling over next. You should now have three layers of dough and two of filling.
10. Roll out the dough again to a rectangle measuring 22 cm (9 in) high x 33 cm (13½ in) wide.
11. Lightly spray the surface with water.
12. Roll up the dough towards you like a Swiss roll and extend to 45 cm (18 in) long. Make sure it is rolled to an even thickness.
13. Using a long, sharp serrated knife cut into nine 5 cm (2 in) buns (use a sawing action to prevent squashing the rolled dough pieces).
14. Place the buns, swirl side up, onto a baking paper lined 25 cm (10 in) round cake pan (preferable at least 5 cm (2 in) deep. One placed in the center and the remaining eight around it.
15. Place in a lidded plastic lidded tub to prove for approximately 45 minutes.
16. When fully proved (Tip 2), remove from the box, Place the pastries on a baking tray and bake at 200°C (400°F) for 15–17 minutes.
17. Remove from your oven and leave in the cake pan to cool down.

Danish Pastries

If you have made the croissant recipe in this book then the procedure is the same for much of this. The recipe is a little different if you compare them, but it is still an enriched yeasted dough. You can make many varieties of Danish pastries but if there is a filling or fruits that you prefer to use then please give them a try.

Makes 8

Ingredients

300 g (10½ oz) white bread flour
300 g (10½ oz) plain (all purpose) flour
7 g (¼ oz) salt
65 g (2¼ oz) caster (superfine) sugar
30 g (1 oz) fresh yeast OR 15 g (⅛ oz) dried yeast
30 g (1 oz) egg (cold)
180 ml (6½ fl oz) milk (cold)
120 ml (4¼ fl oz) water (cold)
300 g (10½ oz) laminating butter

Method

1. Firstly, prepare the laminating butter by rolling out to 20 cm (8 in) high x 25 cm (10 in) wide, using plenty of flour to prevent sticking or place between two sheets of baking paper. Keep in the fridge until ready to use.

2. Weigh all the dry ingredients separately, then place them in a plastic bowl, flour first then the rest in separate piles on top.

3. Add the egg, milk and water, and then combine together until a dough starts to form and the sides of the bowl are clean.

4. Remove the dough from the bowl and knead (Technique 1) on your work surface until it becomes smooth and elastic (approximately 10–12 minutes). This dough does not need to be as fully developed as for a typical bread dough as it will receive further development whilst it is being rolled and folded.

5. Form the dough into a sausage shape and place in a lidded plastic box and leave to rest for 10 minutes.

6. Remove from plastic box and, using a rolling pin, roll out the dough into a rectangle measuring 25 cm (10 in) high x 45 cm (18 in) wide.

7. Place the prepared and cold (but malleable) laminating butter over two-thirds of the dough. Fold into three starting with the surface that has no butter on, making sure the dough and butter layers are separated and no butter is protruding out of the sides.

8. This butter is now incorporated into the dough and three half turns are required.

9. Each half turn means rolling dough to 25 cm (10 in) high x 45 cm (18 in) wide, then folding into three and leaving it to rest for 5–10 minutes. Do this three times and then place back in your lidded plastic box and leave for 20 minutes to rest (in the refrigerator if the butter is very soft or leaking out of the dough).

10. Remove the pastry from the plastic box and gently roll out to 35 cm (14 in) high x 46 cm (18½ in) wide. If you take your time doing this, you will reduce the chances of the butter coming through the dough onto the outer surface, which will make the rest of the process sticky and very difficult to manage, also affecting the finished pastries.

11. Using a pizza roller cutter, trim off the outer edge to neaten the rectangle to 33 cm (13½ in) high x 44 cm (17 in) wide. Cut strips measuring 11 cm (4½ in) high x 44 cm (17 in) wide. You should now have three identically-sized strips.

12. Place one of the strips in front of you in landscape orientation. At the top edge, measure and mark every 11 cm (4½ in). You should have three marks. Do the same with the bottom edge.

13. Now cut (use the pizza wheel) from the bottom to the top in straight lines to divide the strip into four equal squares.

14. Repeat this with the other two strips and you should end up with twelve 11 cm (4½ in) squares of Danish pastry, which you can make into some of the shapes I have describe below. The flavor combinations I suggest can be replaced with whatever you prefer. Once they have been

made into your chosen shapes please refer to the following baking instructions.

15. Always allow room for the pastries to expand on the tray during both proving and baking.

16. Place the tray of Danish pastries into your lidded plastic box to prove for 30–40 minutes. There will be much more expansion in the oven as they bake, than what they will achieve whilst proving.

17. Place on any toppings as described within the instructions for your chosen shapes.

18. Place the proved Danish pastries into your oven and Bake at 200°C (400°F) until golden brown (approximately 15–18 minutes). Pastries with Crème Patissière and fruits on might take a few more minutes to bake fully.

19. Remove the tray from your oven and place on a cooling wire rack to help retain the crispiness of the pastry.

Shape options:

1. Bears Paw–Place: A rope of marzipan (pre-softened a little with some egg whites approximately 2 cm (1 in) in from the top edge and not completely to the sides (or it will pour out in the oven). Brush a little water across the bottom edge and fold over to encase the marzipan. The front edge and sides should have approximately 2 cm (1 in) of pastry stuck together and the back should contain the marzipan. Press the pastry together to seal. Cut three insertions in the front edge but not as far as the marzipan. Place onto a baking tray lined with baking paper ready for proving and baking.

Once baked and cooled, spread some Fondant Icing (page 190) on top and sprinkle on some toasted flaked almonds, then dust liberally with icing (confectioners') sugar.

2. Pin Wheel: Make diagonal cuts from each corner to halfway to the center of each square. Fold the right hand side of each corner to the center and press on top of the previous to keep in place. It should now look like a pin wheel. Place onto a baking tray lined with baking paper ready for proving.

Once proved, pipe a bulb of Crème patissière (page 203) in the center and place some fresh raspberries on top (press in a little so they stay on top during baking).

Once the pastry is baked and cool, paint the top with some boiled apricot jam.

3. Turnover: Place in the filling of your choice (nothing too

liquid) like cooked apples or a pie filling. Avoid placing the filling to close to the edges. Wet the edges and fold over to form a triangle. Press the edges together to form a tight seal. Brush the top with beaten egg and dip in coarse sugar.

Place onto a baking tray lined with baking paper ready for proving and baking.

4. Cushions: Slightly stretch each corner, then fold the point into the center pressing down to secure each one.

Place onto a baking tray lined with baking paper ready for proving.

Once proved, pipe a bulb of Crème patissière (page 203) in the center and then place some cherry pie filling on top (at least five cherries and not too much syrup).

Once baked and cool, spread some Fondant Icing (page 190) onto the top of the pastry, avoiding the toppings.

5. Apricot Half Turnovers: Slightly stretch two opposite corners then fold the point into the center pressing down to secure each one. Leave the other two unfolded.

Place onto a baking tray lined with baking paper ready for proving.

Once proved, pipe a rope of Crème Patissière (page 203) down the center (but not as far as the ends and then place two apricot halves on the Crème Patissière, either side of the center.

Once the pastry is baked and cool, paint the top with some boiled apricot jam.

PAUL'S TOP TIP

You will end up with off cuts of pastry with this recipe. I recommend you make some Monkey Bread (page 158) by cutting strips 1 cm (½ in) wide and 2.5 cm (1 in) long (they do not need to be exact), dipping in melted butter and rolling in cinnamon sugar.

Alternatives to Squares

Instead of making 12 squares from the pastry, you could use it like you would if making Chelsea or Cinnamon Buns. Instead of cutting the final rolled out Danish Pastry into four strips measuring 11 cm (4½ in) high x 44 cm (17 in) wide, you could just cut it in half so you end up with two strips measuring 22 cm (9 in) high x 44 cm (17 in) wide. Each one of these strips you could spread with your choice of filling, roll it up into a sausage and then cut into eight equal portions. Lay them down so the spiral is facing upwards and then prove and bake as for the other Danish pastries.

PAUL'S TOP TIP

Sprinkle some crumble mixture over the top of each fully proved spiral before baking, to give an extra dimension to the pastries. Drizzle some fondant icing (page 190) over them once baked and cool.

Monkey Bread

From something so simple comes something so magic; Monkey Bread. I had not seen this product until I was on holiday in Antigua and loved it immediately. Every day at the breakfast buffet, plates of monkey bread were brought out, and within minutes the plates were empty (literally!). Naturally when I managed to get hold of some for my breakfast, I was instantly analysing it to establish how I could make it back home. Not content with just trying to analyse the monkey bread at the breakfast table, I actually managed to get a shift in the kitchen making the next batch with the chef. So then I left Antigua a happy (and suntanned) man.

The monkey bread is often made in Bundt pans, but can be made in cake tins too. You could also make individual small pans as well. They will freeze really well and can be reheated to serve warm.

Makes: one 23 cm (9 in) Bundt pan and some smaller pans

To make this recipe, use the ingredients from the Danish Pastry on page 152.
You will also need a bowl of melted butter and a separate bowl of cinnamon sugar (4 parts granulated sugar to 1 part ground cinnamon).

Method

1. To make the monkey bread you will firstly need to make a batch of Danish pastry dough using the recipe on (page 152). Follow the method up until you roll out the laminated dough to 35 cm (14 in) high x 46 cm (18½ in) wide. Instead of cutting out squares from the pastry, you will need to cut out strips approximately 1 cm (½ in) wide. Then cut the strips into random sized pieces around 2.5 cm (1 in) long (they do not need to be exact). You will now have a pile of rectangle pieces of Danish Pastry. Even the scrappy outer edge can be used.

2. Grease your Bundt pan and/or other pans using a little white fat on a paper towel.

3. One-by-one, dip a strip of Danish Pastry into the melted butter and then roll immediately in the cinnamon sugar. Then place in the Bundt pan.

4. Continue dipping and rolling the strips, then randomly placing each strip in the Bundt pan until half filled. Repeat with your other cake pans. Don't pile them too high in the Bundt pan as it will become difficult to bake thoroughly.

5. Place the pans in a lidded plastic box to prove for approximately 30 minutes.

6. Place the pans into your oven and bake at 200°C (400°F) until golden brown, approximately 25–30 minutes (or less if using smaller pans).

These will bake quite dark and the top pieces will be crunchy. Monkey Bread is so nice when eaten warm, but is perfectly alright to eat cold too.

Gâteaux Pithivier

A round, puff pastry pie with an apricot and frangipane filling, which classically has scalloped edges, curved cuts on top and a shiny crust when baked. It brings back memories of my college days where I learnt to make this one. You can customize this by adding your own choice of jam, curd or fruits if you wish. You could even 'cheat' and buy some frozen puff pastry if you do not have time to make the following recipe from scratch.

Makes: one 25 cm (10 in) round pie)

Stage 1—Puff Pastry

Note–The frozen puff pastry might not be made with butter and will be inferior to that made with butter.

Ingredients
250 g (9 oz) bread flour
250 g (9 oz) plain (all purpose) flour
50 g (1¾ oz) unsalted butter, softened
300 ml (10½ fl oz) water (cold)
450 g (1 lb) unsalted butter for laminating

You will also require some Apricot jam and Frangipane Filling (see also Raspberry Frangipane page 122)

Method
1. Firstly, prepare the laminating butter by rolling out to 20 cm (8 in) high x 25 cm (10 in) wide, using plenty of flour to prevent sticking or place between two sheets of baking paper. Keep in the fridge until ready to use.
2. Weigh all the dry ingredients separately, then place them in a plastic bowl, both flours first, then the butter.
3. Add the water, and then combine together until a dough starts to form and the sides of the bowl are clean.
4. Remove dough from the bowl and knead (Technique 1) on your work surface until it becomes smooth and elastic (approximately 10–12 minutes). This dough does not need to be as fully developed as for a typical bread dough as it will receive further development whilst it is being rolled and folded.
5. Form the dough into a sausage shape and place it in a lidded plastic box and leave to for 30 minutes.
6. Remove the dough from the plastic box and, using a rolling pin, roll out the dough into a rectangle measuring 25 cm (10 in) high x 45 cm (18 in) wide.
7. Place the prepared and cold (but malleable) laminating butter over two-thirds of the dough. Fold into three, starting with the surface with no butter on, making sure the dough and butter layers are separated and no butter is protruding out of the sides.
8. This butter is now incorporated into the dough and six half turns are required.
9. Each half turn means rolling dough to 25 cm (10 in) high x 45 cm (18 in) wide, then folding into three and leaving for 5–10 minutes to relax. Do this six times (resting the dough between each half turn) and then place back in your lidded plastic box and refrigerate (if necessary) for 10–20 minutes for its final relaxation.

It is not always necessary to place the dough in the refrigerator to rest between each half turn if your table and room are both cold. Ideally the butter and dough are kept similar in consistencies. If the butter becomes too hard it will fracture whilst laminating and you will have inconsistent layering.

10. After resting, remove the pastry from the box and cut just over a third off and roll this piece to approximately 3mm (⅛ in) thick but wide enough to cut a 25 cm (10 in) diameter disc. If you take your time doing this, you will reduce the chances of the butter coming through the dough onto the outer surface, which will make the rest of the process sticky and very difficult to manage, also affecting the finished pastries.

11. Allow 5 minutes for the dough to relax before cutting the 25 cm (10 in) diameter disc, otherwise the cut piece will shrink to an oval shape.

12. Roll the remaining dough to 5 mm (¼ in) thick and wide enough to cut a 27.5 cm (11 in) diameter disc (remember to allow 5 minutes for the dough to relax before you actually cut the disc).

Stage 2—Construction of the Gâteaux Pithivier
Method

1. Place the smaller puff pastry disc onto a baking tray lined with baking paper.

2. Spread apricot jam over the pastry disc but leave 2.5 cm (½ in) from the outer edge clear.

3. Pipe the frangipane filling over the apricot jam, slightly thicker in the middle, avoiding the outer edge too.

4. Brush the outer edge with water and then place the larger pastry disc on top.

5. Gently press to seal the edge and neatly trim away any excess of the top layer.

6. Add a scallop pattern around the edge with your fingers by pushing the pastry edge inwards with one finger whilst gently pressing down with fingers either side, to stop the pastry moving. Continue all the way around the pie.

7. Glaze the top with beaten egg.

8. Score the top surface, with the back of the tip of a knife, from the center to the edge of each scallop on the outside in a curved motion. Do this all the way round. You might find this easier on a turntable.

9. Place in the refrigerator for 30 minutes to relax before baking.

10. Place the tray into your oven and bake at 200°C (400°F) for 40 minutes (until golden brown and crispy in the center).

Laminated Pastries

Millefoglie

A 'thousand leaves' or known simply as a custard slice in English. The Italian and French name sounds more appropriate! Layers of flaky puff pastry sandwiching Crème Patissière, and some fruits too, if you wish. My version has a middle layer of vanilla sponge soaked in orange juice. If you prefer, replace the sponge with a puff pastry layer instead. You need to make sure the Crème Patissière is very thick so it will stay in situ, especially when cut. When I make this in the bakery it is as a long rectangle, and then I cut into portions after the layers have been built up. This is very difficult to cut, therefore you will bake yours as individual pieces to eliminate this 'stressful experience!'

Makes: 8 Millefoglie

Ingredients
To make this recipe, use the ingredients from the gâteaux Pithivier on page 160.
You will also need some Crème Patissière (page 203), some Swiss roll sponge (page 88) and some icing (confectioners') sugar for dusting.

Stage 1—Pastry

Method
1. Using the recipe and method to make the pastry for the gâteaux Pithivier (page 160) but roll the final dough out to 4–5 mm (¼ in) thick, and big enough for three strips of pastry of 10 cm (4 in) high x 40 cm (16 in) wide (although if you use a sponge layer in the middle you will only require two strips).
2. Mark the top and bottom of each strip every 5 cm (2 in) and cut (using a pizza roller) into eight equal portions from each strip.
3. Place them on a baking paper lined baking sheet (you might require two or three) and leave for 30 minutes in the fridge to relax.
4. Place the tray in your oven and bake at 200°C (400°F) for approximately 15 minutes (until golden).
5. Leave them on the tray to cool.

Stage 2– Constructing the Millefoglie

Method
6. If you intend to add any fruits I recommend using berries and placing them on the Crème patissière layers.
7. Lay eight rectangles of baked puff pastry in front of you and trim flat if too puffy.
8. Pipe a layer of Crème patissière on top, slightly in from the edge.
9. Next, if using sponge, cut eight rectangles the same size as the pastry. Lay each one on top of the Crème Patissière and generously brush on some orange juice and allow to soak in. If not using sponge, just lay a second piece of pastry on.
10. Now pipe a layer of Crème patissière onto the sponge (or pastry if used), slightly in from the edge.
11. Finally place a pastry lid on each.
12. Using a sieve, generously dust the tops with icing (confectioners') sugar.

Extra Finishing Touch: If you carefully heat up a skewer over a flame you can 'brand' the top through the icing (confectioners') sugar in a criss-cross pattern. If you have the skewer hot enough it should smoke instantly as it burns the sugar. You will have to keep reheating the skewer to finish all eight.

Eccles Cakes

Contrary to which the name implies, Eccles Cakes are not cakes as like a Victoria Sandwich cake. These are a bakery classic made from a disc of puff pastry in which a dollop of Eccles filling is added and then encased within the pastry, flattened and baked. You could 'cheat' and use a ready made pastry, but if it is not all butter puff pastry then you are not going to make the perfect Eccles Cake.

Makes: at least 10

Ingredients
To make this recipe, use the ingredients from the Gâteaux Pithivier on page 160.
You will also need egg for glazing and Granulated sugar.

Stage 1—Pastry

Method
1. Using the recipe and method to make the pastry for the gâteaux Pithivier (page 160) but roll the final dough out to 3–4mm (⅕ in) thick. It does not matter too much about keeping this into a rectangle as you will be cutting circles from it.
2. Cut out ten 15 cm (6 in) diameter discs.

You can freeze spare discs for another time or make more Monkey Bread (see page 158) by cutting strips 1 cm (½ in) wide and 2.5 cm (1 in) long (they do not need to be exact), dipping in melted butter and rolling in cinnamon sugar. It is also possible to gently rework all the scraps (only once) and cut out some more discs to be used for Eccles Cakes (if you keep reworking the dough it will lose its layers).

Stage 2—Eccles Filling

Ingredients
30 g (1 oz) unsalted butter, melted
150 g (5½ oz) raw (demerara) sugar
175 g (6 oz) currants

2 g (pinch) cinnamon
zest of 1 orange
zest of 1 lemon

Method
1. Carefully melt the butter in a microwave or over a bowl of hot water.
2. Add all the other ingredients to the butter and stir through thoroughly. It should end up as a granular crumble consistency.

Stage 3—Constructing the Eccles Cakes

1. Brush the outer edge of the top of a pastry disc with a little egg.
2. Place a dollop of Eccles filling in the center.
3. Pick up the edges of the disc and squeeze together like a tied up sack and flatten a little with your hand. Turn it over so the rough end is facing down and, using a rolling pin, gently flatten it, but keeping it as a circle (trying not to expel the filling).
4. Brush the top with beaten egg, dip in the granulated sugar and place on a baking paper lined baking tray. Repeat with all your other discs.
5. Using a sharp knife carefully cut two lines in the top (only through the top layer of pastry to reveal some filling).
6. Place the tray in your oven and bake at 200°C (400°F) for approximately 20 minutes (until golden).
7. Remove the tray from your oven and place on a cooling wire rack.

Biscuits and More

In this section I have grouped together Biscuits with other products including Flapjacks, Florentines, Macarons, Scones and Waffles. Biscuits can be quite simple recipes, so always make sure the ingredients are of the finest quality, whereas something like a Macaron, although still requires quality ingredients, is so much more technically challenging to make.

Some of the products in this section are perfect to be used as gifts for birthdays and Christmas. With these products you can also determine the size you wish to make them, especially is they need to fit within any special packaging you might have to be used as gifts.

Scottish Shortbread

Extremely moreish, and synonymously Scottish is this biscuit. Exported all round the world, it's a very basic recipe really, but a high level of butter imparts the classic 'shortness' to the biscuit. The addition of ground rice adds a little crunch when eaten.

Makes: 24 small fingers

Ingredients
100 g (3½ oz) unsalted butter
75 g (2½ oz) caster (superfine) sugar
20 g (⅔ oz) egg
180 g (6½ oz) plain (all purpose) flour
15 g (½ oz) ground rice

Method
1. Place the butter and sugar in a plastic bowl and beat to a light cream.
2. Add the egg and beat in thoroughly.
3. In a separate bowl, mix the flour and ground rice together.
4. Add the flour and rice mixture to the batter and blend through until it just forms a smooth dough.
5. Roll out the dough to a rectangle measuring 22.5 cm (9 in) high x 17.5 cm (8 in) wide, which will be approximately 1 cm (½ in) thick.
6. Dock well (use a docking roller or skewer). Cut into fingers 7.5 cm (3 in) long x 2.5 cm (1 in) wide, which will make 24 pieces.
7. Place on a baking tray lined with baking paper and bake at 190°C (375°F) for approximately 10–12 minutes (without excessive coloring).
8. Remove the tray from your oven and immediately dredge with caster (superfine) sugar.
9. Leave to cool on the baking tray.
10. When cool the shortbread should be crisp and break cleanly.
11. Historically, a carved, wooden block was also used to make a large moulded shortbread. You can buy these quite readily on internet auction sites.
12. Roll out shortbread dough to fit the wooden mould.
13. Dust the wooden mould with ground rice.
14. Place in the shortbread and use the rolling pin to force the dough into the indentation of the mould.
15. Trim off the edges.
16. Turn upside down onto a baking tray lined with baking paper and tap out the moulded dough.
17. Dock the center (use a docking roller or skewer).
18. Using a scotch scraper, you can pre-cut portions (8–10 depending on size of wooden mould), but leave them connected (once baked and cool it is easy to break off equally portions).
19. Place the tray into your oven and bake at 190°C (375°F) for approximately 15–18 minutes (without excessive coloring).
20. Remove the tray from your oven and immediately dredge with caster (superfine) sugar.
21. Leave to cool on the baking tray.
22. When cool the shortbread should be crisp and break cleanly.

White Chocolate and Macadamia Nut Cookies

This recipe makes a soft and slightly chewy cookie. The invert sugar helps to create softness and smoothness when eaten. White chocolate and macadamia nuts makes for a marriage made in heaven. If you prefer another flavor combination then replace the chocolate and nuts in similar quantities with your alternatives. If you cannot obtain any invert sugar, then I have added a recipe for you to make your own.

I normally make this in larger batch sizes and keep it in the fridge for up to six weeks. This means you can bake some whenever you feel like a warm cookie. As this is a soft dough, it is portioned with an ice cream scoop or rolled into balls with your hands rather than rolled out with a rolling pin.

Makes: 14 cookies

Ingredients
190 g (6½ oz) caster (superfine) sugar
110 g (4 oz) unsalted butter, softened
90 g (3¼ oz) invert sugar
vanilla extract, to taste
50 g (1¾ oz) eggs
250 g (9 oz) plain (all purpose) flour
2 g (1 pinch) baking powder
100 g (3½ oz) macadamia nuts
100 g (3½ oz) white chocolate chunks (bakeable)

Invert Sugar Syrup
250 g (9 oz) caster (superfine) sugar
120 ml (4¼ fl oz) water
small pinch Cream of Tartar

Method
1. Place the sugar, butter, invert sugar and vanilla in a plastic bowl and beat together until light.
2. Add the eggs in stages, beating well between each addition.
3. In a separate bowl mix the flour and baking powder together, and then add them to the batter and gently mix until a smooth dough is formed.
4. Add the nuts and chocolate and thoroughly blend through.
5. Using an ice cream scoop, place dollops on a baking tray lined with baking paper (leaving plenty of room for them to spread to approximately 11 cm (4½ oz). Dip the scoop in very hot water (shake off the excess before you collect more dough, and then the dough will slide off easily onto the baking tray. Or, the dough should just be firm enough to roll into balls with your hands. If the dollops of dough weigh approximately 60 g (2 oz) each, you should get 14 cookies out of this recipe.
6. Place the tray into your oven and bake at 180°C (350°F) for 12–14 minutes (soft bake with not much color on top otherwise they will end up too crunchy).
7. Remove the tray from your oven and place on a cooling wire rack. Try to take the cookies off the baking tray as soon as you can to stop them continuing to bake on the hot tray.
8. Place all invert sugar syrup ingredients into a saucepan and bring to the boil and do not stir. Brush the sides of the pan with water to prevent any crystals forming. Continue boiling until the temperature reaches 114°C (237°F).
9. Remove from heat and leave to cool.
10. It is now ready to be used in the cookie recipe.

Millionaires Shortbread

I continue the shortbread theme with this recipe, by producing this wonderful combination of three products; biscuit, caramel and chocolate. This combination is a recognised winner in the biscuit and confection markets. A shortbread base is baked, then smothered with caramel and finished off with a chocolate layer topping. Often this topping is a combination of milk and white chocolate marbled together. You will require a 22.5 cm (9 in) square baking pan.

Makes: 9 squares

Ingredients
To make this recipe, use the ingredients from the Scottish Shortbread on page 166.

Stage 1—Pastry

Method
1. Use the recipe and method for the Scottish Shortbread on (page 166).
2. Roll out the dough to fit your 22.5 cm (9 in) square baking pan.
3. Line the baking pan with a layer of baking paper (bottom and sides and place a layer of shortbread dough inside to fill the bottom (you might need to press the dough into the corners).
4. Place the pan onto a baking tray and bake at 190°C (375°F) for approximately 13–15 minutes (without excessive coloring).
5. Remove the baking tray from the oven and leave to cool.

Stage 2—Caramel Filling

Method
1. Use the recipe for Caramel Filling on (page 197)

Stage 3—Chocolate Topping

Ingredients
250 g (9 oz) milk chocolate (melted)
100 g (3½ oz) white chocolate (melted)
Melt the chocolate and combine in a small bowl until well mixed.

Stage 4—Construction of the Millionaires Shortbread

Method
1. Leave the baked Shortbread base in the baking pan and pour in the Caramel Filling (spread level if necessary).
2. Leave to cool.
3. Pour on the melted milk chocolate to cover the caramel.
4. Randomly spoon on dollops of melted White Chocolate then, using the tip of a knife, swirl the two chocolates to create a marbled appearance.
5. Place into your refrigerator to set.
6. Using the baking paper to hold on to, you should be able to remove the set Millionaires Shortbread from the tray.
7. Using a sharp clean knife, firstly mark into nine portions (3 x 3), then cut through the layers. Clean the knife every time you cut to avoid crumbs or caramel appearing on the chocolate.

Flapjack

A classic flapjack is a relatively simple recipe, which should be a little chewy to eat. If possible, try to obtain jumbo oats (porridge) rather than using breakfast porridge oats which are smaller and dustier. My flapjack is a great base recipe and has just the addition of cinnamon for flavor. So if you remove the cinnamon you can then add other flavors, nuts, cereals, dried fruits and chocolate drops.

Makes: 9 squares

Ingredients
210 g (7½ oz) unsalted butter
210 g (7½ oz) raw (demerara) sugar
210 g (7½ oz) golden syrup (or maple syrup)
380 g (13½ oz) jumbo oats (porridge)
9 g (⅓ oz) ground cinnamon

Method
1. Place the butter in a saucepan and melt on your hob.
2. Add the raw sugar and golden syrup, and bring to the boil, stirring occasionally to prevent the sugar burning.
3. Remove the saucepan from the heat and add the oats and cinnamon. Mix together until thoroughly blended through.
4. Pour into a baking paper lined 23 cm (9 in) square baking pan.
5. Firmly press flat all over; making sure it is an even height.
6. Place the baking pan on a baking tray, Place the pastry on a baking tray and bake at 180°C (350°F) for approximately 20 minutes (it is baked when the edges closet to the tin are golden and the center just starts bubbling).
7. Remove the tray from your and leave to cool in the baking pan.
8. When cool, remove the flapjack from the baking pan and cut into nine squares.

TIP

Dip (diagonally) half of each portion of the cut flapjack into some melted milk chocolate and place in the fridge to set firm.

Florentines

┌─────────────────────────────────┐
│   TIP   │
│   │
│ Try not to get any Florentine crumbs in the │
│ chocolate. If you do, pass the chocolate through a │
│ sieve whilst it is still liquid to remove the lumps. │
└─────────────────────────────────┘

A premium confection containing expensive ingredients but relatively easy to make. Fruits and nuts are caramelized, and when set, their bases are dipped in dark chocolate. The combination of dried fruits and nuts can be changed to suit your preference. You can use all hazelnuts for example, or use dried cranberries for Christmas. Whatever you remove or change, make sure the total amount of nuts and fruits weighs 285 g (10 oz). This helps to keep a balance of fruits and nuts to syrup mixture in this recipe.

I find you get a much nicer-looking Florentine if you bake them within 10 cm (4 in) crumpet rings. After dipping in dark Belgian chocolate I leave them to set on a Silpat (silicone pastry) baking mat, which leaves a honeycomb impression in the chocolate.

Makes: approximately 8 Florentines

Stage 1
Ingredients
80 g (3 oz) unsalted butter
15 g (½ oz) honey
70 g (2½ oz) caster (superfine) sugar
15 g (½ oz) glucose syrup
40 g (1½ oz) whipping cream (or double cream)
70 g (2½ oz) hazelnuts
40 g (1½ oz) toasted flaked almonds
50 g (1¾ oz) pecans
75 g (2½ oz) almond halves
50 g (1¾ oz) raisins

Method
1. You will also need around 500 g (1 lb 2 oz) dark chocolate for dipping the baked Florentines in. You will temper more chocolate than will be used to coat them, but then you can use this chocolate again for something else.
2. Place the butter in a large plastic bowl and melt it to a liquid in the microwave or over hot water.
3. Add the honey, sugar, syrup and cream to the melted butter and mix until thoroughly dispersed.
4. Now add all the nuts and raisins into the bowl and mix these thoroughly into the syrup mixture.
5. Place 8 crumpet rings on a baking paper lined baking tray. Line these rings with a paper bun or Florentine case, or you will need to make your own with baking paper (otherwise the caramel syrup will run underneath the crumpet ring leaving just the fruits and nuts inside the ring).
6. Place dollops of the Florentine mixture in the center of each crumpet ring. Try to add a similar amount in each. Keep stirring the Florentine mixture in the bowl each time you take some out, as this will help keep the heavy nuts and lighter syrup evenly dispersed.
7. Place the baking tray into your oven and bake at 170°C (325°F) for 12–15 minutes (do not let them bake dark brown on top as they will set rock hard, aim for a golden brown color).
8. Remove the tray from your oven, and leave the Florentines to cool on the baking tray.
9. When cool, remove the Florentines from the crumpet rings and take off any baking paper stuck to them. To prepare the Florentines ready for dipping in the chocolate, remove any loose pieces around the edges and discard.

Stage 2—Construction of the Florentines
Method
10. Temper around 500 g (1 lb 2 oz) of dark chocolate (see page 206)
11. Dip the base of each Florentine into the tempered dark chocolate, shake off any excess and place onto your Silpat baking mat with the pattern side up if it has one (use clean baking paper if you do not have a Silpat mat).
12. Leave to set. Place in the fridge for 10–15 minutes to fully set the chocolate.
13. Florentines should easily peel off the mat.
14. Store the Florentines in a cool, dry environment. Never store them in the fridge as they will turn sticky.

Macarons

The classic French meringue, the Macaron (not Macaroon, which is coconut based) has become a global trend. Brightly colored, exquisite flavors and posh packaging sees this product sit alongside premium handmade chocolates in most Patisseries. A mixture of meringue with ground almonds seems rather straightforward. If only!

This is a two-stage process; Italian Meringue and Almond Paste, which requires both stages to be ready at the same time to allow for successful amalgamation.

Makes: approximately 20–30 Macarons depending on the size piped

Stage 1— Italian Meringue

Ingredients
125 g (4½ oz) egg whites
Lemon Juice (few drops or Cream of Tartar (pinch)
220 g (7¾ oz) caster (superfine) sugar
60 ml (2 fl oz) water

Method
1. In a grease-free bowl, whisk egg whites (aged and at room temperature).
2. Add either lemon juice or Cream of Tartar to the egg whites to strengthen the foam.
3. Whilst the meringue is whisking, boil the caster (superfine) sugar and water in a saucepan (without stirring) until 118°C (245°F).
4. Slowly pour the boiled sugar into the whipped egg whites (whilst still whisking) and continue whisking on medium speed until cool. If you stop whisking before the meringue cools, it might well collapse.
5. Add any paste coloring to the Italian meringue whilst cooling.
6. Whilst the meringue is cooling make the almond paste.

Stage 2— Almond Paste

100 g (3½ oz) egg whites

250 g (9 oz) icing (confectioners') sugar
250 g (9 oz) ground almonds

Method
1. Sieve the icing (confectioners') sugar and almonds together a couple of times to remove any large pieces of almond.
2. Add the egg whites until a thick paste is formed.
3. Gradually add the Italian Meringue to the thick Almond Paste and gently fold together (Technique 8–please read this before folding these together).
4. Keep folding until the mixtures are completely combined and the consistency is that similar to volcanic lava.

   Important Note–Be careful not to overwork this as it will become too runny and the Macarons will flow excessively.

5. Using a plastic piping bag or use a large strong freezer bag (Tip 7) pipe discs (Technique 10) 3 cm (1½ in) 5 cm (2 in) onto baking paper (placed on two baking trays and leave for approximately 20 minutes to form a skin). Lightly tap the tray to release air bubbles.
6. Leave for approximately 20 minutes to form a skin on top before baking.
7. Place the tray in your oven and bake at 150°C (300°F) to 160°C (325°F) for approximately 10–12 minutes. To check whether the macarons are baked, gently lift the corner of the baking paper and try to peel the closest macaron away from the paper. If it resists (or the center is still stuck), leave

to bake for a couple more minutes. If it just about peels away from the paper, then remove the tray from the oven and leave to cool.

8. The macarons must not show any signs of browning of the crust. If they do, they will be overbaked and therefore crunchy, not chewy inside.

Stage 3—Finishing your Macarons

Method

1. Macarons are sandwiched together using strongly flavored buttercreams, ganache, jams or curds. You can be really creative with your colors of the Macarons and flavors used inside. Fillings with high moisture contents like ganache will soften the Macaron quicker than if using a buttercream. But this will take a few days to significantly soften. Ganache is a great filling though, as the texture is very smooth and it incorporates liqueurs easily. There are a few possible filling recipes in this book for you to get creative with (see page 183).

Sort your baked macarons into similar-sized pairs. Turn one of each pair over so the base is facing upwards. Pipe your chosen filling onto the macaron and then place its matching pair on top, with a gentle twist to secure it.

TIPS

* When filling the bag with the macaron batter, let the batter fall off the spatula and then gently add more. Do not scrape the spatula clear of batter each time you add to the bag, as this damages the batter making it liable to flow too much after piping onto the tray.
* Draw circles on the baking paper to use a guides before piping the macaron discs. Turn the paper over before piping, otherwise the pen mark will appear on the base of the baked macaron.

TIPS

* To get creative, use different colored Macarons for the top and bottom; chocolate and orange for example. You can also use a complimentary buttercream and jam or curd layer inside.
* After piping your Macarons, place a few nibbed or flaked almonds, sugar pearls or other finely chopped nuts on top. This will create a visual difference to the normal finish once baked. Only decorate half of them, and leave the undecorated ones for use as the bottom of the sandwiched Macarons. If the decorated ones are used underneath, they do not sit flat on a tray when presented.

Scones

If you've only ever made one baking product in your life, I bet it was a scone! Well, that might not apply to everyone, but I'm pretty sure it does to most. A scone, still warm from the oven and filled with jam and clotted cream, is, albeit a relatively simple product, somewhat warming and homely, like the classic Victoria Sandwich.

Traditionally buttermilk is used in conjunction with bicarbonate of soda to raise the scone. My recipe uses baking powder instead. You are more likely to have baking powder in your cupboard than to have buttermilk in your fridge. Cut out whatever sized scones you like, the process is just the same as the baking time will vary by a minute or two).

Makes: approximately 10–12 Scones depending on size chosen

Ingredients
135 g (4¾ oz) plain (all purpose) flour
410 g (14½ oz) bread flour
120 g (4¼ oz) caster (superfine) sugar
2.5 g (pinch) salt
25 g (1 oz) baking powder
135 g (4¾ oz) unsalted butter, softened
265 ml (9½ fl oz) milk

Method
1. Place both flours, sugar, salt and baking powder in a plastic bowl, and mix them together until nicely dispersed.
2. Add the butter and blend through the powders until thoroughly dispersed.
3. Add the milk and blend this through until a dough is formed.
4. Split dough into two, gently round into balls and cover.
5. Leave the dough for 10 minutes to relax.
6. Using a rolling pin, gently roll one of the balls until 1.5 cm (½ in) thick.
7. Cut out discs of dough and place on a baking paper lined baking tray.
8. Brush the tops of each piece of dough with some beaten egg. Avoid spilling the egg down the sides of the dough as it will burn at the base of the scone whilst baking.
9. Leave the dough pieces to relax for 15 minutes before baking.
10. Place the tray of scones in your oven and bake at 200°C (400°F) for approximately 15 minutes. The should be golden brown on top and golden on the sides.
11. Leave to cool on the baking tray.

TIPS

* Dip the cutter into flour before you cut out each scone. This will help produce a neat and clean cut, which will help the scone to rise evenly.
* Next time you visit the DIY store, purchase a length of 1.5 cm (½ in) thick baton. Cut into two even length sticks, which fit nicely on your work surface. Roll out the scone dough between the sticks, with the ends of the rolling pin resting on them. This will ensure that the scones will all be made to the same thickness.
* sultanas are often used in scones and can be added to the recipe above. I recommend adding 125 g (4 oz). It is also beneficial to pre-soak and thoroughly drain the sultanas before adding them to the dough. This makes the baked scone extremely moist to eat. However, be careful not to overwork the dough as the sultanas will be soft and liable to break apart.

Gingerbread

This recipe is ideal for making small gingerbread biscuits. Alternatively if using this to make structures like a gingerbread house, replace the plain (all purpose) flour with bread flour to impart more strength. The use of the bakers' blackjack caramel imparts color to the gingerbread. If you cannot obtain this then use black treacle or caramel color. Both will give color, but at different strengths. The lemon zest is optional. I add the lemon as it works well with the heat from the ginger.

Makes: approximately 10–12 small biscuits

Ingredients

200 g (7 oz) plain (all purpose) flour
65 g (2¼ oz) raw (demerara) sugar
2 pinches bicarbonate of soda
7 g (¼ oz) ground ginger
85 g (3 oz) unsalted butter, melted
35 ml (1¼ fl oz) golden syrup (or maple syrup)
5 g (⅕ oz) Blackjack caramel
zest of 1 lemon

Method

1. Place the dry ingredients into a plastic bowl, flour first then remaining ingredients on top.

2. Blend together until thoroughly dispersed.

3. In a separate bowl melt the butter, either carefully in a microwave, or over hot water.

4. Add the syrup, blackjack caramel and lemon zest to the melted butter and stir through.

5. Finally, add the liquids to the blended powders and mix until a dough forms.

6. Using a rolling pin, gently roll the dough out to 5 mm (⅕ in) thick.

7. Cut out desired shapes and place on a baking paper lined baking tray.

8. Place the tray in your oven and bake at 180°C (350°F) for approximately 15 minutes (depending on the size of biscuits cut from the dough).

9. When baked, remove the tray from your oven and leave the gingerbread to cool on the tray.

TIP

If making structures like houses, the edges of the gingerbread can be trimmed straight with a serrated tomato knife after baking.

Chocolate Orange Almond Biscuits

From this mix you should end up with lots of mini, soft almond biscuits, which will go perfectly with an espresso after dinner. Keep them in a Kilner jar and they should keep for a week. The biscuit mixture is piped onto a tray and therefore the mixture's consistency should be soft, but when you pipe the discs they should not flow. When baked, the biscuits should be soft to eat and so they are not in the oven for very long.

Makes approximately 30 biscuits

Ingredients
75 g (2½ oz) egg
175 g (6 oz) caster (superfine) sugar
110 g (4 oz) ground almonds
20 g (⅔ oz) unsweetened cocoa powder
zest of 1 orange

You will also need some bakeable chocolate chunks for decoration.

Method
1. Place all ingredients in a plastic bowl and blend together with a wooden spoon until thoroughly blended through. The mixture should be thick, but pipeable (similar to a Macaron consistency).
2. Place the mixture into a plastic piping bag or use a large strong freezer bag (Tip 7). Cut a 5 mm (¼ in) hole and pipe 1 cm (½ in) discs of the mixture onto a baking paper lined baking tray, allow a little room for them to spread.
3. Place a bakeable chocolate chunk on the top of each one.
4. Place the tray into your oven and bake at 170°C (325°F) for 6–8 minutes.
5. The biscuits should be soft after cooling, so be careful not to bake them with too much color forming.

TIP

If the mixture is too runny, blend in some more ground almonds to stiffen it.

Viennese Biscuits

These biscuits should literally melt-in-the-mouth when eaten. Although it is mixed to a dough, it will be soft enough to pipe. A star n ozzle is traditionally used to pipe fingers, shells or rosettes. Once they are baked, matching pairs of biscuits are sandwiched together with jam or buttercream or both and can also be dipped in chocolate.

Ingredients
225 g (8 oz) unsalted butter, softened
75 g (2½ oz) white fat
105 g (3¾ oz) caster (superfine) sugar
30 g (1 oz) egg (room temperature)
vanilla extract, to taste
190 g (6¾ oz) bread flour
190 g (6¾ oz) plain (all purpose) flour
buttercream

Extra icing (confectioners') sugar, a jar of strawberry jam and some melted chocolate is required for finishing the Viennese.

You will also need to make half of the buttercream recipe on page 200.

Method
1. Place the butter, white fat and sugar into a grease-free plastic bowl and beat together with a wooden spoon until 'light' and 'fluffy' (see page 223).
2. Next add the egg (a third at a time) and beat in thoroughly. There is only a small amount of egg so it will not curdle.
3. Add both flours to the batter and mix thoroughly to make sure there are no lumps or areas of the batter that have no flour (you can see these as they will be darker in color to that which has the flour incorporated). The final batter should be thick but pipeable (more like a paste).
4. Place the mixture into a plastic piping bag or use a large strong freezer bag (Tip 7) fitted with a star n ozzle in the end.
5. Pipe your chosen shapes on a baking paper lined baking tray, leaving a little space in between each piped shape as they will expand a small amount in your oven.
6. Place the tray into your oven and bake at 170°C (325°F) for approximately 12–15 minutes (depending on the size of biscuits piped). The biscuits will be a light golden brown color at the edges and creamy gold in the middle when baked.
7. Remove the tray from your oven and, if possible, slide the paper containing the Viennese off the tray and onto a cooling wire rack. This will stop them from baking any further on the hot tray.
8. When cool, pair them up into equal sizes and turn one of each pair over.
9. Pipe some jam or buttercream (or both) onto the flat surface of the one you turned over.
10. Place its pair on top (don't press it down too hard as the biscuit might break).
11. Finishing can be as simple as lightly dusting with icing (confectioners') sugar, or dipping the ends in melted chocolate or drizzling melted chocolate across the tops.

TIPS

* If you are making different size biscuits from the same batter, then I recommend that you pipe them on separate trays so you can achieve the perfect bake for each size made.
* If you pipe rosettes, they classically have half a glace cherry placed on top before baking. Only place a cherry on every other one. The ones without the cherry will be the base of the biscuit when sandwich together after baking.

Fillings and Toppings

The recipes in the section are used when making multi-component desserts, tortes and many other patisserie products.

Some of these are complete desserts within themselves, but you can get creative and modify them to suit yourself as components.

Not all of the ones here are referred to within the recipes in the book. They are here so you can use them within your creative baking at home. So when you need a filling or topping then choose one from this selection rather than searching the internet.

Liqueur Filling

Get creative with you own flavor combination with this recipe by using orange and Grand Marnier, Lemon and Limoncello, Coffee and Baileys for example. Choose your ideal combination and use them at the levels in the recipe. The filling can be used in pastry cases as for Tarte au Citron, injected into cupcakes or as a layer in a cake or a mousse.

Makes approximately 355 g (12½ oz)

Ingredients
100 g (3½ oz) unsalted butter

Juice of ½ orange or 1 lemon or 1 espresso shot (omit the zest if using coffee)

zest of 1 orange or of 2 lemons

125 g (4½ oz) icing (confectioners') sugar

70 g (2½ oz) egg yolk

25 g (1 oz) egg

25 ml (1 fl oz) liqueur (your chosen flavor)

Method

1. Firstly, melt the butter in a large saucepan until a liquid, and then add the fruit zest and juice (if used) plus the icing (confectioners') sugar. (The sugar with turn lumpy after it has been added to the melted butter. Don't worry, as this will dissolve whilst heating up).

2. Bring this liquid to a boil, stirring randomly.

3. Mix the egg yolk and whole egg together (plus espresso–if used) in a separate large plastic bowl.

4. Carefully, pour the boiled liquid into the eggs, stirring continuously.

5. It might thicken slightly at this point, but will undoubtedly require further heating.

6. Continue to cook (stirring continuously to prevent burning) the mixture, either back in the pan or in the microwave (30 second increments until it becomes thick. There is more chance in the mixture burning if placed back on the stovetop to thicken. You need this to be thicker than a lemon curd at this point because once the liqueur has been added it will soften to the correct consistency.

7. Add your choice of liqueur and stir through.

8. Set aside to cool.

Vanilla Bavarois

A Bavarois is a mousse but without meringue incorporated, so is therefore slightly heavier in texture. Made the same way by making a Sauce Anglaise (custard) adding gelatine to set it and folding in whipped cream (a mousse would now have meringue added too). Flavoring and colors can be added to this if desired (add them at the point when the gelatine is stirred into the Sauce Anglaise).

Makes approximately 900 g (31 ¾ oz)

Ingredients
25 g (1 oz) leaf gelatine
300 ml (10½ fl oz) milk
100 g (3½ oz) yolk
75 g (2½ oz) caster (superfine) sugar
400 g (14 oz) whipping cream
vanilla extract, to taste

Method
1. Soak the leaf gelatine in a little water and set aside.
2. Place the milk in a saucepan and bring to the boil.
3. In a separate bowl blend the egg yolk and sugar together.
4. Add the boiled milk to the egg yolk and sugar mixture and stir through.
5. Place this mixture back into the saucepan and continue heating (and stirring) until it thickens enough to coat the back of a spoon (do not boil as it will separate).
6. Remove the soaked gelatine from the water and, together with a few drops of vanilla extract, place into the custard mixture and stir through until dissolved.
7. Set aside to cool and until it is almost set.
8. In a separate bowl whisk the cream until fully whipped.
9. Gently fold the whipped cream into the cooled custard mixture and avoid over mixing.
10. It is now ready to pour into your Bavarois ring, or into glasses if making individual desserts.

TIP

If using a metal ring, place a plastic film strip around the inside edge before adding the freshly made Bavarois. This will allow the ring to be removed easily once the Bavarois has set.

Chocolate Bavarois

A Bavarois is a mousse but without meringue incorporated, so is therefore slightly heavier in texture. Made the same way by making sauce Anglaise (custard) adding gelatine to set it and folding in whipped cream (a mousse would now have meringue added too). You will require some top quality dark chocolate. The higher the cocoa solids content in your chosen chocolate, the stronger the flavor will be in your Bavarois.

Makes: 1kg (35 ¼ oz)

Ingredients
25 g (1 oz) leaf gelatine
300 ml (10½ fl oz) milk
100 g (3½ oz) yolk
75 g (2½ oz) caster (superfine) sugar
100 g (3½ oz) dark chocolate (melted)
400 g (14 oz) whipping cream
vanilla extract, to taste

Method
1. Soak the leaf gelatine in a little water and set aside.
2. Place the milk in a saucepan and bring to the boil.
3. In a separate bowl blend the egg yolk and sugar together.
4. Add the boiled milk to the egg yolk and sugar mixture and stir through.
5. Place this back into the saucepan and continue heating (and stirring) until it thickens enough to coat the back of a spoon (do not boil as it will separate).
6. Remove the soaked gelatine from the water and place into the custard mixture and stir through until dissolved.
7. Add the melted chocolate and stir through thoroughly.
8. Set aside to cool, and until it is almost set.
9. In a separate bowl whisk the cream until fully whipped.
10. Gently fold the whipped cream into the custard mixture and avoid over mixing.
11. It is now ready to pour into your Bavarois ring, or into glasses if making individual desserts.

TIP

If using a metal ring, place a plastic film strip around the inside edge before adding the freshly made Bavarois. This will allow the ring to be removed easily once the Bavarois has set.

Orange Mousse

This mousse is used within the 'orange', our award-winning pastry. A mousse is lighter than a Bavarois due to the meringue addition at the final stage of the process. Its texture is extremely light and bubbly. You can use this mousse to make your own dessert by using it as a layer in a torte or pipped into a glass with a layer of dark chocolate ganache for example.

Makes approximately 340 g (12 oz)

Ingredients
5 g (⅕ oz) leaf gelatine
125 ml (4½ fl oz) milk
30 g (1 oz) yolk
40 g (1½ oz) caster (superfine) sugar
juice of ½ orange
zest of 1 orange
65 g (2¼ oz) whipping cream
50 g (1¾ oz) egg whites

Method
1. Soak the leaf gelatine in a little water and set aside.
2. Place the milk in a saucepan and bring to the boil.
3. In a separate bowl blend the egg yolk and sugar together.
4. Add the boiled milk to the egg yolk and sugar mixture and stir through.
5. Place this back into the saucepan and continue heating (and stirring) until it thickens enough to coat the back of a spoon (do not boil as it will separate).
6. Remove the soaked gelatine from the water and place into the custard mixture and stir through until dissolved.
7. Add the orange juice and zest and stir through.
8. Set aside to cool and until it is almost set.
9. In a separate bowl whisk the cream until fully whipped.
10. In another grease-free bowl whisk the egg whites until it makes soft peaks (add a little Cream of Tartar or lemon juice before it is completely mixed to strengthen the foam).
11. Gently fold the whipped cream into the custard mixture.
12. Finally, gently fold the egg white foam into the mixture trying not to damage the egg whites.
13. Place in the refrigerator until ready to use or pour into your moulds or dessert glasses.

Bread and Butter Pudding Sauce

This sauce is ideal for making bread and butter pudding or alternatively you can experiment with using up old croissants, brioche or panettone. Basically if whatever you have is sweet and yeasted and going stale, then you can give it a new lease of life by making a pudding with them. The recipe contains cream to impart richness to the pudding. The recipe is enough for a small pudding approximately 20 cm (8 in) square. If you need more, it is a simple recipe to increase the quantities or make a second batch.

Makes: enough for approximately one 20 cm (8 in) square dish.

Ingredients
240 g (8½ oz) egg
140 g (5 oz) caster (superfine) sugar
300 g (10½ oz) whipping cream
300 ml (10½ fl oz) milk

Method
1. Cut your chosen sweet breads into slices (as like thick sliced bread) and lay them in a buttered baking dish.
2. Place the eggs and sugar in a plastic bowl and beat together until thoroughly mixed through.
3. Pour in the cream and milk whilst stirring until a well-mixed liquid is achieved.
4. Pour on the pudding sauce and let it soak in for a couple of minutes. Add some more until it is completely soaked.
5. Ideally it is baked in a water bath (place the dish in a roasting pan with some water in it; half to two-thirds up the sides of dish) to prevent the pudding sauce from splitting.
6. Bake at 170°C (325°F) for 40–60 minutes (depending on how thick you have made your pudding). The pudding sauce is set when it is a 'wobbly' consistency.
7. Remove the pudding dish from your oven and allow to cool a little before cutting in to it.
8. Dust with icing (confectioners') sugar before serving.

TIPS
* When placing your chosen breads in the baking dish you could also add dried fruits, berries and nuts before pouring on the pudding sauce.
* Make an adult version by blending some bourbon whiskey into the pudding sauce before pouring over your choice of breads. Use 55 g (2 oz) to the recipe above.

Italian Meringue

There are different ways to make a meringue. The Italian meringue involves using boiled sugar. This produces a more stable and smoother meringue with a better shelf life. This is my preferred method of making meringues and I use this method when making macarons. It might sound a little daunting having to boil sugar and add to whisked egg whites simultaneously, but it really is not that difficult as long as you have a thermometer.

Use this recipe whenever you require meringue within a dessert or if you just want to make some meringue shapes to bake.

This size recipe fits nicely in a standard domestic food mixer with whisk attachment.

Makes approximately 500 g (1 lb 2 oz)

Ingredients
150 g (5¼ oz) egg whites (room temperature)
juice of 1 lemon (few drops or Cream of Tartar (pinch)
250 g (9 oz) caster (superfine) sugar
100 ml (3½ fl oz) water

Method
1. Whisk the egg whites in a grease-free bowl.
2. Add either lemon juice or Cream of Tartar to the egg whites to impart strength to the foam.
3. As the meringue is whisking, boil the caster (superfine) sugar and water in a saucepan (without stirring) until 118°C (245°F).
4. Slowly pour the boiled sugar into the whipped egg whites (whilst still whisking) and continue whisking on medium speed until the meringue is cool. If you stop whisking before the meringue cools, it might well collapse.

TIP

If you require the meringue to be colored, add the coloring at the cooling down stage. You will need to scrape the sides of the bowl after you have added the color, as you will notice this part of the meringue is still white.

Fondant Icing

To decorate many bakery products, fondant icing is used. Not to be confused with the fondant roll icing (sugar paste) which is used to cover celebration cakes, fondant icing is more like a super-saturated sugar. I described it as like a fudge icing without any fat in it. I use it a lot on Danish pastries, Swiss finger buns, frangipanes and fondant fancies. In the baking trade I can purchase a solid block of fondant, which requires a little water, heat and plenty of stirring to achieve the correct consistency. Unfortunately this is not readily available for home bakers. There are a couple of options you can use instead.

Firstly, you can purchase powdered fondant icing (confectioners') sugar in supermarkets. This is icing (confectioners') sugar blended with dried glucose. It allows for a thicker, smoother icing than icing (confectioners') sugar alone achieves. You add a little water to the sugar and stir to make a thick icing. It can also be colored and flavored too.

Alternatively, you can break down the fondant roll icing (sugar paste) with a little water. This makes something close to the consistency of a bakers' fondant icing but, a little less glossy and a different taste.

Makes approximately 545 g (19 ¼ oz)

Ingredients
500 g (1 lb 2 oz) white fondant roll icing (sugar paste)
45 ml (1½ fl oz) water (warm)

Method
1. Using an electric mixer with a beater attachment, slowly break down the sugar paste (added in small chunks with the water added slowly. It will be a bit lumpy to start with, but it will come together to a smooth thick icing eventually. You can vary the water content slightly to adjust the fondant consistency.

Arrowroot Glaze

A fruit tart should look stunning and create a wow when presented, but if glazed it can add another dimension, especially when using vibrant colored fruits. The bright colors are enhanced and the light reflecting off the shiny glaze catches the eye. But not only does the glaze enhance the visual aspect, it also has a practical use as it helps protect the fruit from shrivelling up and browning.

You can use this glaze to cover the fruits used on Danish Pastry and frangipanes too.

If you use water in the recipe, the glaze will be the most transparent. Alternatively by using fruit juices you can add some flavor to the glaze but it will introduce some color to it.

Makes approximately 330 g (11½ oz)

Ingredients
30 g (1 oz) arrowroot
300 ml (1 fl oz) water or apple juice

Method
1. Blend the arrowroot with a little water or juice to form a lump-free paste, and then add the remaining liquid.
2. Place in a saucepan and heat, whilst stirring continuously.
3. As it gets close to boiling it will start to thicken and become translucent.
4. Remove from the heat and leave to cool, or use straight away by brushing onto the fruit.

If the glaze is too thick to brush on a neat coating, add a little more liquid until the consistency is better.

Royal Icing

Many people will just guess the amount of icing (confectioners') sugar to egg whites to make royal icing but this is very hit and miss when they do that and when it finally looks the correct consistency they might have twice as much as they anticipated. Royal icing has a recipe like everything else, therefore if you follow it you will achieve the perfect consistency first time. If you are covering a cake with the royal icing it must be free from air bubbles and if you are using it to write with, it must be lump-free to get through the tiny nozzles.

Nowadays, coating cakes with royal icing is less popular and actually, a lost art; generally now being replaced by the sugar paste roll icing. Even writing with it has been replaced with letters being tapped out of a special type of sugar paste instead.

The addition of glycerine allows for the icing to be soft setting. If omitted, the icing will be rock hard when set.

Makes approximately 650 g (23 oz)

Ingredients
85 g (3 oz) egg whites
550 g (19½ oz) icing (confectioners') sugar
15 g (½ oz) glycerine

TIP

If stored in the fridge, allow the royal icing to come back to room temperature before using, as it will feel hard and not spread. Do not add more egg whites to it when it feels hard due to being cold, as this will make it too soft as it warms up; possibly after you have used it.

Method
1. Place all ingredients into a grease-free bowl and stir together, then mix for about 10 minutes. It is easiest to do this using a food mixer with the beater attachment on slow speed.
2. To test when the icing is the correct consistency, insert a spatula and then remove. The icing should be drawn to a point as the spatula is removed.
3. Once made, the bowl of royal icing must always be kept covered with a damp cloth to prevent it from forming a crust. Even when you are using it, keep it covered as much as possible. Also keep the sides of the bowl clear of icing as these bits will harden extremely quickly. If you do find any hard bits, then they should not be mixed into the good icing; throw them away.
4. Any remaining unused icing should be stored in an airtight container and placed in the refrigerator for up to three days, as it contains raw egg.

Crème Brûlée

A great crème brûlée needs a rich recipe, and this one works perfectly. A traditional French origin dessert comprising of a heavy, creamy custard with a hard, caramelized sugar topping. It can also have fruit fillings too. It can be served at room temperature but my preference is to eat it when the custard is really cold and the hard caramel topping is still hot. I like to savor the contrast between the two.

Makes: 6 medium ramekins—9 cm (3½ in) diameter

Ingredients

500 g (1 lb 2 oz) whipping cream
75 g (2½ oz) caster (superfine) sugar
50 g (1¾ oz) egg
100 g (3½ oz) egg yolk
vanilla extract, to taste

Method

1. Heat the cream in a saucepan until hot, but not boiling (if it does boil, just leave the cream to cool for a couple of minutes).

2. In a separate bowl mix the sugar and egg together.

3. Whilst stirring continuously, pour the hot cream into the sugar and egg mixture. Keep stirring until thoroughly blended through.

4. Pour in the liquid into your ramekins until they are half full (approximately 120 g (4¼ oz).

5. Place them in a roasting tray and fill with water until half way up the sides of your ramekins.

6. Place the roasting tray in your oven and bake at 170°C (325°F) for approximately 20 minutes until just set. Time will vary depending on the depth of filling in your ramekins. The Crème Brûlée is set when it is a 'wobbly' consistency.

7. When set, remove the roasting tray from your oven and leave to cool down in the water. When cold enough to touch, then remove them (without dripping water on the others and allow to thoroughly cool down.

8. Place the baked crème brûlée in the fridge until ready to serve.

9. To serve, sprinkle a layer of caster (superfine) sugar on top.

10. Then, either place under a hot grill, or use a blowtorch to caramelize the sugar. Stop when it darkens and is bubbling.

TIP

If using a blowtorch, keep it moving over the surface of the sugar layer to help achieve an even and gradual browning. Do not hold it too close either as the flame could be too fierce. After you have caramelized a couple of the individual crème brûlée, you should have the technique perfected.

Crème Brûlée Macchiato

I invented this dessert to be used in our afternoon tea selection when Cinnamon Square appeared on *Britain's Best Bakery* television series. As Cinnamon Square is a bakery and coffee shop I thought this product encompassed these two areas really well. It was well received by the judges and can remember one of them tasting it, and then passing his comments about it to the camera, then coming back and polishing the remainder off!

It is based on the classic Crème Brûlée, but contains Belgian chocolate and espresso, which turns this wonderful rich dessert into something extra special. Instead of ramekins, I use espresso glasses. This allows them to be more visual and clearly highlights the coffee aspect. Rather than caramelizing sugar on top, a foam layer is applied to replicate the froth. I then dusted cocoa powder on top through a miniature stencil of the Cinnamon Square logo.

Makes: 8 espresso glasses

Ingredients
250 g (9 oz) whipping cream
40 g (1½ oz) caster (superfine) sugar
25 g (1 oz) egg
50 g (1¾ oz) egg yolk
60 ml (2 fl oz) espresso
45 g (1½ oz) dark chocolate (melted)

Method
1. Heat the cream in a saucepan until hot, but not boiling (if it does boil, just leave the cream to cool for a couple of minutes).
2. In a separate bowl mix the sugar and egg together.
3. Whilst stirring continuously, pour the hot cream into the sugar and egg mixture. Keep stirring until thoroughly blended through.
4. Now add the espresso and melted chocolate to the mixture and blend through thoroughly.
5. Pour in the liquid into your espresso glasses until half full (approximately 55 g (2 oz).
6. Place them in a roasting tray and fill with water until half way up the sides of your espresso glasses.
7. Place the roasting tray in your oven and bake at 170°C (325°F) for approximately 30 minutes until just set. Time will vary depending on the shape your espresso glasses. The Crème Brûlée Macchiato is set when it is a 'wobbly' consistency.
8. When set, remove the roasting tray from your oven and leave to cool down in the water. When cold enough to touch, then remove them (without dripping water on the others and allow to thoroughly cool down.
9. Place in the fridge until ready to apply the foam topping and serve.

Stage 2—Foam Layer
Ingredients
80 g (3 oz) egg whites (room temperature)
juice of 1 lemon
pinch of Cream of Tartar
2 g (1/14 oz) leaf gelatine
25 g (1 oz) water

Method
1. Place the gelatine in a small bowl, pour in the water and leave to soften.
2. In a grease-free bowl, whisk egg whites.
3. Add either lemon juice or Cream of Tartar to the egg whites for adding strength to the foam.
4. Place the bowl containing the gelatine in the microwave to gently warm and dissolve (don't let it get hot).
5. Fold the dissolved gelatine through the egg whites trying not to damage the foam.
6. Using a spoon, lay some of the foam on the top of each set macchiato to look like a frothy layer.
7. Using a fine strainer, dust a little cocoa powder over the foam and serve.

Crumble Topping

Crumble toppings are just a simple blend of flour, sugar and butter. Oats, nuts, and spices can be added (as in the Canadian Coffee Time Cake (page 105), as well as using darker sugars and flours. If replacing any ingredients, keep the quantities the same, if adding extra ingredients it will be a bit trial and error. This crumble topping is ideal to use on top of fruits to make a fruit crumble. It can also be sprinkled on cakes and on choux or sweet pastry before baking to impart a crackled layer on top when baked.

Makes approximately 410 g (14 ½ oz)

Ingredients
200 g (7 oz) plain (all purpose) flour
130 g (4½ oz) caster (superfine) sugar
80 g (3 oz) unsalted butter, softened

Method
1. Place the flour and sugar in a plastic bowl and mix together.
2. Add the butter and rub through the dry ingredients until a crumble is formed.

TIP

If adding spices, use 8 g (¼ oz) and for oats and nuts, start by adding 55 g (2 oz) to the recipe above. Whatever addition level you end up with, and are pleased with the results, make a note for next time.

Caramel

Heating cream or milk, sugar and butter together eventually makes a thick, golden, smooth sauce. The longer it is heated for, the thicker it will become and harder it will set. You can add salt, to taste, if you prefer to make a salted caramel version.

Makes: enough for a 23 cm (9 in) square tray for Millionaires Shortbread

Ingredients
160 g (5½ oz) unsalted butter
85 g (3 oz) raw (demerara) sugar
600 g (1 lb 5 oz) condensed milk

Method
1. Using a heavy-bottom saucepan, place all the ingredients inside and gently heat them together until the butter is melted.
2. Bring to the boil and then, whilst stirring continuously to prevent the caramel burning on the bottom of the pan, continue cooking on low heat for at least 5 minutes.
3. The caramel should slowly turn a rich golden brown color and thicken.
4. At 110°C (230°F) the caramel should be ready.
5. Either dip the base of the pan in cold water to stop the caramel from cooking further, or pour immediately onto the biscuit base if making Millionaires Shortbread.

Creams

In this section I have added various creams; from a basic buttercream, which is ideal for coloring and flavoring to the more high end patisserie-style Swiss Meringue Buttercream, which uses a longer process to make, but ends up as an extremely silky, smooth-textured cream.

Buttercream

Many basic buttercream recipes contain 2 parts sugar to 1 part butter (and often a little milk). This makes a heavy and 'sickly' buttercream and the addition of milk not only compromises the shelf life but can often make it too sloppy to use. My recipe replaces some of the butter with white fat. This allows the buttercream to be beaten to a lighter texture and also makes it more pleasant to eat. It is whiter in appearance, which allows for colors to be added.

Makes: 1 kg (2 lb 4 oz) of buttercream

Ingredients
500 g (1 lb 2 oz) icing (confectioners') sugar
250 g (9 oz) unsalted butter, softened
250 g (9 oz) white fat
vanilla extra, to taste

Method
1. Place the sugar, butter and white fat in a plastic bowl and gently blend all the ingredients together.
2. Add any colors and flavors and beat the buttercream until a light texture.
3. For a chocolate buttercream, add 100 g (3½ oz) melted, dark chocolate.

TIP

The cream is generally beaten to a light consistency, which is ideal for layering the inside of cakes and for topping cupcakes. However, for covering the outside of a cake, which you might need a smooth finish then I recommend mixing it slowly and not for too long. This will produce a buttercream with less air bubbles inside, which allows for a smoother finish when applied using a pallet knife.

Coffee Buttercream

The only way to make a great coffee-flavored cream is to use top quality espresso shots. It is just not the same if you use flavorings instead. Also, the espresso delivers the perfect color to the cream naturally. We use this recipe to decorate our coffee and walnut cake and coffee cupcakes. If you cannot make espresso at home, don't worry; just buy a takeaway double espresso from your favorite local coffee shop, covered to keep in the aroma and used as soon as humanly possible!

Makes: enough to sandwich and decorate a 22.5 cm (9 in) round cake.

Ingredients
600 g (1 lb 5 oz) icing (confectioners') sugar
250 g (9 oz) unsalted butter, softened
250 g (9 oz) white fat
55ml (2 fl oz) espresso (cold)

Method
1. Place the sugar, butter and white fat in a plastic bowl and gently blend all the ingredients together.
2. Add the espresso, and beat the buttercream until a light texture.

TIP

If the buttercream is too fluid for your intended use, I recommend adding more icing (confectioners') sugar to control the thickness. Add 25 g (1 oz) at a time. Stir through thoroughly and evaluate before adding any more.

Marshmallow Buttercream

This recipe uses marshmallow fluff to impart a different texture and flavor to the buttercream.
I use it on some of my cupcakes and also as the filling for my Whoopie Pies. It is rather sweet so it would not be best suited to use in layer cakes.

Makes approximately 900 g (2 lb)

Ingredients
75 g (2½ oz) white fat
75 g (2½ oz) unsalted butter, softened
300 g (10½ oz) marshmallow fluff
450 g (1 lb) icing (confectioners') sugar

Method
1. Place the fat, butter and marshmallow into a large plastic bowl and stir together until thoroughly blended.
2. Add the icing (confectioners') sugar and stir through. Slowly beat the ingredients together for a couple of minutes until smooth.
3. Add any colors and flavors and mix through.

TIP

In the warmer months the frosting might be too soft to use, especially if intending to pipe shapes with definition (rosettes on top of cakes with it. Therefore I recommend increasing the amount of icing (confectioners') sugar in the recipe by 15 per cent - 67 g (2½ oz) to make it firmer.

Cupcake Frosting

This makes a heavy cupcake frosting and forms a touch-dry outer surface. It is ideal to be colored and flavored, and when piping with n ozzles it will retain a sharp definition. It uses ready made fudge icing in the recipe, which can be purchased in most supermarkets.

Makes approximately 715 g (1 lb 9 oz)

Ingredients
450 g (1 lb) vanilla fudge icing
75 g (2½ oz) unsalted butter, softened
190 g (6½ oz) icing (confectioners') sugar

Method
1. Place the fudge and butter into a large plastic bowl and stir together until thoroughly blended.
2. Add the icing (confectioners') sugar and stir through. Beat all the ingredients together slowly for a couple of minutes until smooth.
3. Add any colors and flavors and mix through.

TIP

If the fudge icing is too firm to stir, soften it before use as for the butter.

Swiss Meringue Buttercream

Swiss Meringue Buttercream is a high-end patisserie cream, which uses a longer process to make but will end up as an extremely silky smooth textured cream. It is extremely rich due its high fat content, and the lightly cooked meringue creates the ultra-smooth texture, synonymous with this cream.

Makes approximately 715 g (1 lb 9 oz)

Ingredients
160 g (5½ oz) egg whites
275 g (9¾ oz) caster (superfine) sugar
450 g (1 lb) unsalted butter, softened

Method
1. Whisk the egg whites in a large clean grease-free bowl over a pan of simmering water using an electric hand whisk.
2. Gradually add the sugar whilst the egg whites are whisking.
3. Keep whisking the meringue for up to 10 minutes until it feels silky, not grainy when rubbed between fingers.
4. Remove the meringue from the heat and continue to whisk until the meringue is cool (room temperature) and thickened.
5. Add small lumps of the unsalted butter, softened, whisking well between each addition. Gradually it will start to look like a cream.
6. Before you get to the end of adding the butter, you might notice a sudden dramatic change in the texture and appearance of the cream. Stop whisking and place the cream in your food mixer with the beater attachment and continue mixing and adding the butter until all of it is incorporated.
7. You should now have a silky smooth Swiss Meringue Buttercream ready to use.

Cream Cheese Frosting

This is a wonderful recipe to make a cream cheese frosting that has many uses. I use it on some of my cupcakes, Guinness, red velvet, carrot and passion cakes. I also use this on my signature Cinnamon Square Buns, where the frosting is then eaten warm.

Makes approximately 865 g (1 lb 15 oz)

Ingredients
180 g (6½ oz) cream cheese
85 g (3 oz) unsalted butter, softened
600 g (1 lb 5 oz) icing (confectioners') sugar

Method
1. Place the cream cheese and butter in a plastic bowl and mix together until combined.
2. Add the icing (confectioners') sugar to the cream cheese and butter and blend in. Continue mixing slowly until smooth and there are no signs of any lumps.
3. The frosting can be stored at ambient for 5 days.

TIPS

* If using a food mixer with beater attachment to mix this, be careful not to mix it for too long as the cream cheese will break down and the frosting will become too soft to use for most applications.
* In the warmer months the frosting might be too soft to use, especially if intending to decorate cakes with it. Therefore I recommend increasing the amount of icing (confectioners') sugar in this recipe by 15 per cent to 90 g (3$^{1}/_{5}$ oz).

Crème Patissière

I use this recipe a lot as it makes a wonderful rich, creamy custard that has many uses—from something as simple as pouring on top of your apple crumble for your dessert, to filling choux pastry balls to make a profiterole tower. My recipe uses wheat flour to set the custard rather than corn flour. The wheat flour does create a slightly different mouthfeel to that made if using cornflour (cornstarch). By increasing the flour content in this recipe you can produce a thicker custard, to use in Millefoglie for example.

Makes approximately 760 g (1 lb 10 oz)

Ingredients
120 g (4¼ oz) egg yolk
50 g (1¾ oz) caster (superfine) sugar
40 g (1½ oz) plain (all purpose) flour
250 ml (9 fl oz) milk
250 g (9 oz) whipping cream
50 g (1¾ oz) sugar
vanilla extract or ½ vanilla pod, to taste

Method
1. Mix the yolks, sugar (1) and plain (all purpose) flour together in a large bowl.
2. Heat the milk, cream, sugar (2) and vanilla until boiling.
3. Whilst stirring, pour some of the boiled mixture into the egg, sugar (1) and flour blend to loosen the mixture.
4. Now pour in the remaining boiled mixture whilst continually stirring. This mixture should thicken a little as you stir.
5. Either place the mixture back on the stovetop (stirring to avoid burning the bottom layer), and continue heating to thicken, or use the microwave in 20-second blasts stirring each time.
6. The consistency should be thick, but pourable.
    I recommend that you finish the thickening process in a microwave to avoid burning the custard.
7. The Crème Patissière can be kept for three days in a refrigerator.
    For a really thick Crème Patissière, increase the plain (all purpose) flour by 50 per cent to 60 g (2 oz) and proceed exactly as above.

Chocolate

I am sure I do not need to write about how wonderfully indulgent chocolate is to eat and the amazing creations that we can make from it. What I do want to cover in this section is how easy it can be to work with chocolate and how to get the best from it. As I'm sure you're aware, chocolate, especially top quality chocolate, is expensive, so we don't want to waste any! Now it might seem a little daunting at first, but if you read through this section a couple of times and make sure you have all the correct tools in place, I am confident that you will master working with chocolate rather quickly.

WORKING WITH CHOCOLATE

I teach a chocolate course at Cinnamon Square and the objective is to learn why and how we temper chocolate and, at the same time, to make a range of chocolates drawing from a variety of techniques.

So why temper?

If you have ever melted chocolate before, you might well have used some lovely Belgian chocolate that has a wonderful shine to the surface, snaps when broken apart and does not melt in your hands. After melting this over a bain-marie or in the microwave, you end up with a beautiful glossy viscous liquid chocolate. Now, if you then filled a plastic bunny mould for example and left it to set, it would. However, it would set significantly differently to how it had started off before you melted it. It would firstly be stuck inside the mould, as it would not have contracted away from the surface. It will have a dull appearance rather than a glossy shine and will quickly melt in your hands if you hold it. It will eventually form a white dusty coating to the surface (fat bloom) and it would not have the signature 'snap'. This is all because it was not tempered after it was melted.

The cocoa butter, which is the principle natural fat in chocolate, can be seen to comprise two different fat molecules that set at different temperatures. The Fat A form has a low temperature setting and the Fat B form sets at a slightly higher temperature. The Fat A form is the one which we want to avoid, whereas Fat B will impart the characteristic contraction, snap and gloss we require.

Tempering is a process that involves following a specific temperature regime with the chocolate, which will promote the unique Fat B to be the dominant one as it resets after being melted. If you are only a couple of degrees centigrade out from this temperature regime, the wrong fat form (Fat A) will dominate and the chocolate will set with the totally wrong characteristics.

Therefore, a thermometer is VITAL for achieving perfect tempering of your chocolate.

Correct tempering will impart the right qualities of:

- Contraction
- Snap
- Gloss
- Shelf Life
- Color

As well as:

- Correct Melting Characteristics
- Absence of Fat Bloom
- Correct Eating Quality

How to temper

There is more than one method of tempering chocolate. The one I use and teach involves cooling the chocolate on a marble or granite table (or slab). To me, this is the real 'craft' way of doing it and, although can be a little messy, it is an enjoyable experience. Another method is called 'seeding'. This is where chocolate is melted and then small pieces of solid chocolate are added to seed the melted chocolate with the correct fat crystals. Chocolate tempered from either method will be used in the exact same way. I will now focus on the first method.

The principle of tempering on the table

I feel I need to explain the principle of the method first, before you read through the detailed instructions below. The chocolate is heated to make sure all the fat crystals are melted. Most of the chocolate is then poured on the table to cool down, leaving a small proportion of warm chocolate in the bowl. When the chocolate is cooled to the correct temperature on the table it is placed back in the bowl with the warm chocolate and mixed together to even out the temperature. The cooled chocolate should now rise slightly in temperature to the maximum working temperature. It is now ready for making chocolates.

TIP

Make sure you have planned exactly what you are going to make from your tempered chocolate and have it all at arm's reach. This is because when the chocolate is correctly tempered you are on limited time before the chocolate solidifies too much that you cannot make anything from it. When that happens, you will have to start again and re-temper.

Detailed instructions for tempering chocolate

Melt your chosen chocolate—minimum 500 g (1 lb 2 oz)—in a plastic bowl using a microwave (check and stir every 30–60 seconds). It will probably take 2 minutes before it starts to melt.

Both milk and white chocolate contain milk powder which is susceptible to burning when heated too intensely.

When the chocolate reaches the 'Melted Temperature' (see the table below), pour four fifths of the chocolate onto your work surface (preferably marble or granite) and keep the remaining chocolate in the bowl (scrape down the sides of the bowl).

Spread the chocolate over the surface of your table. The more chocolate that is in contact with the marble surface the faster the cooling of the chocolate. Keep the chocolate moving to prevent uneven cooling and to help the formation of the correct fats. Scrape the chocolate back to the middle and check its temperature. Spread it out again, then bring it back to the middle and recheck the temperature. Keep repeating this process until you reach the required 'Cool on Table Temperature' (see the table below).

When the chocolate has reached the required temperature, scrape it back into the plastic bowl containing the remaining warmer fifth of chocolate, and mix together thoroughly to even out the temperature.

Now check the temperature of the mixed chocolate, which should be no more than the 'Maximum Working Temperature' (see the table page 208).

Before using this freshly tempered chocolate, you need to carry out a quick test to see if it is correctly tempered. This will save you a lot of time (and chocolate) if you find it is not tempered correctly. To do this, follow the stalagmite test described below.

The stalagmite test

Drizzle a little tempered chocolate onto some baking paper and leave for a couple of minutes to start setting. Using your index finger touch the top of the chocolate and slowly lift it up. If you can make a stalagmite with the chocolate then it will be tempered and you can start using it. However, if the chocolate flows back down then leave a little longer and try again. If after 5 minutes it is still not making a stalagmite, then you will undoubtedly need to re-temper.

Temperature ranges for correct tempering of chocolate

Chocolate Type	Melted Temperature		Cool on Table Temperature		Maximum Working Temperature	
	°C	°F	°C	°F	°C	°F
Dark (55 per cent Cocoa/Cacao)	45–50	113–122	28–29	82.4–84.2	31–32	87.8–89.6
milk (33.5 per cent Cocoa/Cacao)	40–45	104–113	27–28	80.6–82.4	30–31	86–87.8
White (28 per cent Cocoa/Cacao)	40–42	104–108	25–26	77–78.8	28–29	82.4–84.2

The above temperature ranges might vary slightly according to the brand of chocolate used. If you go over the maximum working temperature, unfortunately you will have to re-temper the chocolate. The per cent cocoa refers to the amount of the cocoa bean present in the chocolate. The remainder will be made up from mostly sugar, milk powder, vanilla and emulsifier. Cocoa and Cacao are alternate forms of the same word and effectively mean the same thing and different brands of chocolate will arbitrarily use the same word.

Tools required

There are a few tools I recommend for successful tempering of chocolate at home.

- Digital Thermometer
- Chocolate Scraper
- Crank Handle Pallet Knife
- Marble or Granite Slab
- Chocolate Moulds
- Plastic Microwaveable Bowl
- Plastic Curved Bowl Scraper
- Chocolate Moulds
- Piping Bags

The room environment is also very import for successful tempering at home. Ideally, if the room is between 15–18°C (59–64.5°F) it is perfect for tempering and setting of the chocolate. If your room is 25°C (77°F) plus, then it is too warm to temper chocolate.

TIPS

* Chocolate moulds are expensive so you need to get creative. You can use anything that is smooth and food grade to be a chocolate mould. A great example is the plastic pot used for individual Christmas or sponge puddings. After cleaning, this could be lined with chocolate, and once set and removed from the pot; it should make the perfect edible dessert cup, which could be filled with a chocolate mousse for example.
* When the chocolate is nearly set, place the chocolate mould in the fridge for 10 minutes to help the chocolate to contract and set.
* If you use plastic transparent moulds it is easy to judge when the chocolate is ready to take out as it will appear translucent through the plastic when set. You can purchase two types; one is made from polycarbonate and is very robust, whereas the other is made from thin plastic which is not so durable but much cheaper.
* Make sure your chocolate moulds are polished clean with a soft cloth before use. This will ensure that the maximum gloss is achieved to the chocolate which is in contact with the surface of the mould, and will also help prevent the chocolate sticking inside the mould.
* Have a bowl of hot soapy water with a cloth and scouring pad close by, you will need it!

Figurines

You can purchase many different moulds of animals, cars, shoes, hearts, Easter eggs, snowmen, Santas and many more. They are constructed from two plastic halves which are either:

A) made separately and then stuck together when removed from the moulds, or

B) clipped together and filled either as a solid piece of chocolate or some chocolate is poured out to make a hollow chocolate shape.

Moulds which contain a lot of detail are best painted with tempered chocolate first and then you can layer a thicker coating underneath. This helps brings out as much detail as possible form the mould. Another option is to use colored chocolate to paint specific details to the mould before applying the bulk of the chocolate.

The inside of the moulds will become the exterior of the chocolates being made. So make sure the moulds are highly polished inside and your painting is neat.

TIPS

* Apply a thin coat to the moulds first and leave them to set. Then add a second layer of chocolate, rather than applying one thick layer in one attempt.
* When a mould is to be hollow, keep the chocolate moving inside by turning the mould round and round for a couple of minutes. This will help form an even coating inside the mould. Before it is completely set, stand the mould upright on some baking paper to allow the remaining liquid chocolate to run down to seal the base.
* When the chocolate is nearly set, place the chocolate mould in the fridge for 10 minutes to help the chocolate to contract and set.

Filled chocolates

There are endless shape designs and flavor combinations possible when making filled chocolates. The main thing to consider though is what the filling is made from. It must have a long shelf life and not contain moisture otherwise the chocolate will spoil very quickly. Ganache and fondant-based fillings work really well.

To make filled chocolates, firstly fill the moulds with tempered chocolate and then pour out the excess, scrape the top clean and leaving to set. Next you need to pipe in your choice of filling, making sure it does not protrude above the height of the mould. Leave the filling to firm a little and then finally fill the remainder of the mould with tempered chocolate and scrape the excess chocolate off the surface of the mould. Leave to set.

Turn the mould over and twist slightly to release the chocolates.

Chocolate lollipops

Just like the filled chocolate moulds, there are many types of lollipop moulds including hearts, animals, Easter and Christmas variations. You will also need the correct size lollipop sticks to fit the moulds. Chocolate lollipops are always solid chocolates and they can be painted inside with different colored chocolate.

To make the lollipops, pipe the tempered chocolate into the moulds with the sticks in situ. Make sure you cover the end of each stick in chocolate so it is embedded. When all the shapes in the mould are filled, tap the mould a few times on the table to release any air bubbles and to also level the chocolate.

Try to fill the shapes within the mould to just below the top level of the indentation. Tap the mould on the table to level the chocolate. If there is room, you can add a little more and re-tap the chocolate flat. If you overflow the indentation the shapes will have a web effect to them once removed from the mould.

Nutty discs

These impressive looking chocolates are really simple to make, as long as you are organised and have everything ready to use at arm's length. These nutty discs are akin to a chocolate version of a Florentine. If they are made approximately 3–4 cm (1–1½ in) in diameter they can then be packed into half a dozen or one dozen for example to make a special gift. The choice of toppings is up to you. I would recommend using dried fruits, peel, cranberries, glace cherries and nuts (almonds, hazelnuts, pecans, pistachio). Do not use anything with a short shelf life or high moisture content as they will spoil too quickly. If you use glacé fruits, make sure you remove the syrup.

You can use dark, milk or white chocolate as the base. I like to use the dark chocolate for its richness, but if you use just cranberries for example, they look nice in contrast to the white chocolate.

How to make nutty discs

Place the tempered chocolate into a plastic piping bag or use a large strong freezer bag (Tip 7).

Cut a 5 mm (¼ in) hole and pipe 3 cm (1 in) discs of chocolate onto a baking paper lined baking tray, allow a little room for then to spread (piping them on a tray is useful, as you can move them out of the way before they are set, so you can make some more).

Place your chosen fruits and nuts on the top of each one. Press them in a little, so they are imbedded in the chocolate.

Leave somewhere cool to set, ideally between 15–18°C (59–64.5°F).

Milk Chocolate Ganache

This ganache is the most versatile flavor of the three as it is not too bitter, nor too sweet and therefore eaten by adults and children. I use it mainly for chocolate celebration cakes, éclairs and profiterole toppings.

Makes approximately 745 g (1 lb 10 oz)

Ingredients
250 g (9 oz) fresh whipping cream
375 g (13 oz) milk chocolate
120 g (4¼ oz) glucose syrup (optional, but it adds a nice gloss to the ganache)

Method
1. Place the glucose syrup in a bowl that's large enough to hold all of the ingredients mixed together.
2. Place the cream in a saucepan and bring to the boil.
3. In a separate bowl, gently melt the chocolate in a microwave, or over a pan of hot water, as in a double-boiler arrangement.
4. Pour the boiled cream, into the glucose syrup, stirring continuously until the glucose syrup is dissolved.
5. Then pour melted chocolate into the boiled cream and glucose syrup mixture, stirring continuously until the mixture is the consistency of a thick cream.
6. Cover and set aside to cool and start setting.
7. If you intend to pipe the ganache, cool it a little in the refrigerator first.

Dark Chocolate Ganache

This is very rich and therefore smaller quantities are used within products. I use it for the filling in my Tarte au Chocolat, as a layer in a Bavarois, as a filling within a chocolate or for covering a Sacher Torte. I would say it is more of an adult ganache.

Makes approximately 920 g (2 lb)

Ingredients
400 g (14 oz) whipping cream
400 g (14 oz) dark chocolate
120 ml (4¼ fl oz) glucose syrup (optional, but it adds a nice gloss to the ganache)

Method
1. Place the glucose syrup in a bowl that's large enough to hold all of the ingredients mixed together.
2. Place the cream in a saucepan and bring to the boil.
3. In a separate bowl, gently melt the chocolate in a microwave, or over a pan of hot water, as in a double-boiler arrangement.
4. Pour the boiled cream, into the glucose syrup, stirring continuously until the glucose syrup is dissolved.
5. Then pour melted chocolate into the boiled cream and glucose syrup mixture, stirring continuously until the mixture is the consistency of a thick cream.
6. Cover and set aside to cool and start setting.
7. If you intend to pipe the ganache, cool it a little in the refrigerator first.

White Chocolate Ganache

I find this very sweet when eaten on its own, and therefore would use it in combination with other products. It is great for making kids celebration cakes with as it can be colored and flavored too. If intending to color it, remember that the ganache will be cream colored when made, not white, and therefore the colors can be affected by this (adding blue will turn slightly greenish).

Makes approximately 650 g (23 oz)

Ingredients
200 g (7 oz) whipping cream
400 g (14 oz) white chocolate
50 g (1¾ oz) glucose syrup

Method
1. Place the glucose syrup in a bowl that's large enough to hold all of the ingredients mixed together.
2. Place the cream in a saucepan and bring to the boil.
3. In a separate bowl, gently melt the chocolate in a microwave, or over a pan of hot water, as in a double-boiler arrangement.
4. Pour the boiled cream, into the glucose syrup, stirring continuously until the glucose syrup is dissolved.
5. Then pour melted chocolate into the boiled cream and glucose syrup mixture, stirring continuously until the mixture is the consistency of a thick cream.
6. Cover and set aside to cool and start setting.
7. If you intend to pipe the ganache, cool it a little in the refrigerator first.

Truffles

You can make many different variations in flavors, shapes and finishes with truffles. Use the three ganache recipes in this book as your starter recipes. Once you get used to making them, you can then start developing your own variations. The basic principle to making truffles is to pipe shapes with the ganache and let them harden in the fridge. The firm ganache shapes are then dipped in chocolate and rolled in one of many varieties of coatings; from cocoa powder to toasted flaked almonds. The ganache itself can be flavored and also contain liqueur.

To make truffles you firstly need to make your ganache, and then leave it until firm enough to pipe shapes with or roll balls in your hand. Pipe 2.5 cm (1 in) fingers of ganache onto trays lined with baking paper and place them into your refrigerator to harden. Whilst in the fridge, prepare your tempered chocolate and place your choice of toppings (i.e. toasted flaked almonds into a tub. When the ganache fingers are hard, place one on a fork, dip into tempered chocolate and then gently shake off the excess. Drop it into your tub full of topping, and roll it to completely cover the truffle. Leave it in the tub to harden before removing it.

> **TIP**
>
> By using the same ganache shapes, but then dipping them into different chocolates and rolling them in different toppings you can create a wide variety of truffles in one go.

Chocolate Covering Glaze

This is ideal for covering a cake to leave a lovely smooth shiny glaze, packed full of chocolate flavor. It is made similar to a ganache but has the addition of leaf gelatine. By using chocolate with higher cocoa solids content, you will increase the flavor intensity and darken the glaze.

Makes approximately 590 g (21 oz)

Ingredients
155 g (5½ oz) milk
60 g (2 oz) glucose syrup
2.5 g (⅒ oz) leaf gelatine
375 g (13 oz) dark chocolate

Method
1. Soak the gelatine in some cold water.
2. Place the milk in a saucepan with the glucose syrup and bring to the boil.
3. Remove the gelatine from the water, squeeze out the excess and add to the boiled milk and stir through until thoroughly dissolved.
4. In a separate bowl, gently melt the chocolate in a microwave, or over a pan of hot water.
5. Pour the melted chocolate into the boiled milk, stirring continuously.
6. Pour into a clean bowl, cover with plastic wrap and leave to cool.

Chocolate Bavarois Cup

This is an idea to use a combination of some of my chocolate recipes to make a rich dessert for the chocoholic. You will need to find a container suitable for making a tempered chocolate bowl or cup, by using a cappuccino cup, plastic beaker or small Christmas pudding basin for example. When you have made some of these you can then build up layers to produce a dessert.

Method
1. Firstly, make your tempered chocolate cups and remove them from their containers (try not to touch the outside of the chocolate with your bare hands as they will leave fingerprints).
2. Pipe a layer of Dark Chocolate Ganache (page 212) in the base.
3. Place some raspberries on top of the ganache.
4. Pipe a thicker layer of Chocolate Bavarois (page 186) on top of the raspberries to just below the top rim of the chocolate cup, and place in your refrigerator to set.
5. When the Bavarois has set, remove from your refrigerator and pour on the Chocolate Covering Glaze (page 215), filling to the top of the cup.
6. When the glaze has firmed up a little, place a plump raspberry on top and serve.

CHOCOLATES WITH THE KIDS

Once you have mastered how to temper chocolate, then you have to get the children involved too. I teach chocolate making to children at Cinnamon Square, and yes, it could be a little messy at times but they gain so much from it and interestingly, show a lot of creativity and care in their work.

I get them involved in every stage of the process. They can see and feel the chocolate initially in its solid form being heated and changing to a liquid, and then using the thermometer to record temperatures during this process. Working the chocolate on the table requires their focus and hand control. Testing the chocolate to judge if it is tempered correctly requires some decision making and then making the chocolates brings out their creativity.

I get them to pipe the chocolate into moulds or directly onto baking paper. A good tip here is to place an elastic band around the top of the piping bag to prevent the chocolate from pouring out onto the floor, whilst they focus on controlling the chocolate coming out of the other end! The kids also really enjoy adding inclusions, toppings and sprinkles to their creations. So have plenty of these available.

I generally use milk and white chocolate when teaching the children but surprisingly many younger children actually seem to like dark chocolate too.

Figurines

If you have moulds to make bunnies and snowmen for example, they make a good activity for the kids. You can remove the set figurines and then carry on decorating them with sweets, edible glitter or paint (food coloring).

Bars

If you have chocolate bar moulds the kids can add sweets to the mould then pipe chocolate on top to fill the mould, or place the sweets on once piped. They can be themed for an occasion like Halloween for example.

Kiddie Discs

As like the Nutty Discs (see page 211) but using plenty of sweets, the kids will really like this one. They could use fruits and nuts, but the preference is generally for the sweets. This is a good opportunity for them to pipe other shapes or write their name (joined up writing) with the chocolate.

Chocolate Pizzas

Using a very clean non-stick cake pan approximately 20 cm (8 in) diameter, the kids can make a chocolate to look like a pizza by firstly pouring in a layer of chocolate then adding grated white chocolate as the cheese. jam could be added for the sauce and they could make other ingredients from colored sugar paste like tomatoes, pepperoni, and mushrooms for example. The toppings must be in contact with some liquid chocolate to stick on top.

Dipped Strawberries

Choose some nice plump strawberries preferably with a good size green calyx in place as this will be what you will hold on to when dipping them into the chocolate. White chocolate looks great against the red strawberry. When dipped, shake off the excess and place onto a baking paper lined plate and leave to set. You can also drizzle dark chocolate over the white chocolate for extra visual appeal.

To give them extra wow, firstly make some dark chocolate discs 3–4 cm (1–1½ in) diameter and leave them to set. After you dip each strawberry, place it on the disc of dark chocolate and leave to set stuck to the dark chocolate disc. These could be served as is, or placed on top of a cake for decoration.

TECHNIQUES

TECHNIQUE 1—Kneading

Kneading forms gluten, providing the elastic properties to the dough, which enables it to expand and hold on to its shape. One of the most common mistakes in home baking is under-kneading, which leads to a weak dough and a heavy bread. Therefore thorough kneading of the dough should not be underestimated. Kneading requires intense stretching and folding of the dough until it becomes smooth and elastic. Do not take this lightly, it is more of a workout than a light therapeutic session!

A series of pictures is required to explain the kneading technique (as shown above)

TECHNIQUE 2—Shaping

Shaping the dough not only provides a visual attractiveness but also imparts strength to the dough; helping to achieve a loaf which is robust and will not collapse before baking. The sausage/cylinder shape is probably the most common used especially in tin loaves and bloomer-style breads.

A series of pictures is required to explain the shaping of the dough (example shown above)

TECHNIQUE 3—Knead testing–The windowpane method

To test whether a dough is fully kneaded you will need to notice that the dough has become smoother, elastic and less tearing occurs as you knead. The windowpane test is your final quality control test. Take a small piece of dough and roll it into a ball and leave it to rest for a minute. Now flatten the ball between your fingers and then gently stretch the dough until you can see through it without tearing (like a balloon expanded to the maximum). This indicates a good level of gluten development; therefore the dough is thoroughly kneaded.

TECHNIQUE 4—Kneading wet dough

Kneading of a wet dough requires a different technique to that of a typical firmer bread dough. Turn out the wet mixture onto the table and knead until smooth and elastic, using the dough using the 'slapping' and 'stretching' action, which is very different from the traditional kneading method.

Hold the dough in the air so that it is hanging downward. Whilst continuing to hold the dough, slap the bottom half against the work surface and then stretch and fold the remaining dough that you are holding over the top of the dough touching the table. Immediately pick up the dough with both hands from the left or right end and let it hang downwards. Repeat the slapping and stretching action. After a few attempts you will find the 'rhythm'. Now keep this going for at least 10 minutes.

Use the windowpane test (Technique 3) to check if the dough is fully developed. This should stretch way more than the bulk-fermented split tin dough.

TECHNIQUE 5—The ribbon stage

The ribbon stage is achieved when eggs are fully whisked and a thick foam is formed. Using the tip of the whisk you should be able to let the foam fall off the whisk in a figure eight shape and it should stay proud of the rest of the batter underneath. The initial egg and sugar liquid will also have changed into a much lighter color and to a thick foam, that is at least three times greater in volume than the original liquid.

TECHNIQUE 6—Testing the cake set

To test whether a cake is set in the oven before you remove it, firstly do not test it with a knife as it will collapse in the center if inserted too soon. Use your finger to test the cake by feeling how springy the outer edge is and then slowly working your way inwards. If it starts to feel softer as you get closer to the center then it needs more baking. When it finally feels springy in the center, give it a few more minutes baking—just to be sure. If your oven is too hot or you positioned the cake too high up, you might notice the cake has darkened too soon. If you place some baking paper over the top it will help prevent the cake from getting burnt, whilst continuing to allow it to bake inside.

TECHNIQUE 7—Cutting the cake in half

To successfully cut a cake in half and in a straight line you need to have a long bladed knife, 30 cm (12 in) preferably. Holding the knife horizontally, half way up against the side of the cake, score the outer edge by turning the cake in a circle, but keep the knife steady in the same place. At the same time, gently move the knife backwards and forwards in a sawing motion. By the time you complete a circle you should meet up with where you started. Now keep turning the cake and moving the knife. You will be gradually cutting your way through to the middle of the cake. Just make sure that the knife stays within the initial cut. When you eventually reach the center of the cake, the top should now be separated. It is important to keep a sawing action with the knife, rather than pushing it through the cake as you will then achieve a cleaner cut through the cake. You will find that the cake is more robust if you chill it before cutting it.

TECHNIQUE 8—Incorporating a meringe into a paste without deflation

This is the method I recommend to incorporate meringue into a paste without deflating it as in macarons or chiffon cake.

You will require a curved, plastic scraper or a flexible, plastic, curved spatula. Place a small portion of meringue into the bowl of paste and using a figure of eight motion, scrape down the inside of the bowl right down to underneath the paste, lift up through the paste, turn the scraper/spatula over and press through the top of the batter. That whole movement should feel like the figure eight. Turn the bowl a quarter turn and repeat this motion. The first addition of meringue will break down, but it will start to soften the paste and a batter will now begin to form. Keep adding the meringue and give a few figure of eight stirs between each addition.

You do not need to thoroughly disperse the meringue each time before you add the next amount, as by the time you have completely added the meringue, most if it will be already now be thoroughly mixed in.

For macarons this batter should be lump-free, of consistent color throughout and it should flow like molten lava. For chiffon cake the batter should also be lump-free, of constant color throughout and the consistency should be airy and thick but will flow slowly when poured into the baking pan.

TECHNIQUE 9—Rolling out sweet puff pastry

To roll out sweet pastry successfully there are a few points to note. If lining a baking foil or pan, use only enough paste to line one foil or pan at a time. Try to keep the paste the same shape of the pan you are lining then you won't have lots of unwanted paste overhanging the pan and tearing off, leaving some of the pan uncovered. The advantage of my sweet pastry recipe is that you can seamlessly patch up any gaps. When rolling the paste, keep the surface lightly dusted with flour (bread flour disperses better) rather than one heavy coating. Always roll from the middle out then back to the middle. Rotate the pastry a quarter turn, then roll again. This paste is soft, so the weight of the rolling pin might be enough pressure. Aim for 3–4mm (1/7 in) thick when lining your cases. As you get experienced using the pastry you will be able to get them thin, but for the first go don't stress too much if they are a little thick. If you are lining a large tin, you might find the pastry a bit difficult to pick up, especially if the pastry is thin. Try using some flat scrapers or fish slices to slide underneath the pastry to pick it up. If there's someone around you could ask for help as three hands are definitely better than two for this job). Trim off the top edge with a knife. Use a slicing action starting from the bottom of the blade through to the top and this will give you a neatly cut edge. Use a fork to dock the bottom of the paste to allow steam to escape whilst baking.

TECHNIQUE 10—Piping

To pipe bulbs of choux paste or macarons, it is important that you first hold the piping bag vertically and then clasp the bag with your hands positioned so that your thumbs are on top, rather than twisting your hand upside-down so your thumb is pointing downwards (which many people naturally do whilst on my courses). With the tip of the bag approximately 5 mm (¼ in) or higher (depending on depth of bulb required) above the tray, start piping. Keep the n ozzle in the center and let the paste flow on its own. Do not start making a circle by moving the bag. When the paste makes the size of circle you are aiming for, stop squeezing the bag and 'flick' the n ozzle away from the center. Just make sure when you do this the n ozzle is 'skimming' the surface of the paste and not buried within it. Allow space between each bulb you pipe for expansion as they bake in the oven.

TIPS

1. Rather than covering the dough with a damp tea towel and placing in the airing cupboard, I recommend using a large clear plastic lidded storage box. This creates a perfect draft-free environment for dough to rise. A cup of hot water can be placed inside to create a little warmth and humidity, which yeasted dough enjoy.
2. To test when dough is fully proved, press the top of the dough gently with the tip of your finger. If it springs back firmly then the dough requires further proving. When it stays slightly indented then the dough is ready for baking.
3. Paint the inside of your baked pastry shell with melted white chocolate and allow to set before adding the Crème Patissière when making fruit tarts. This will provide a moisture barrier between the pastry and the filling cream, which will help to prevent the pastry going soft.
4. Add 15 g (½ oz) of glucose syrup to every 100 g (3½ oz) ganache, whilst still hot, to give increased shine and prolonged shelf life.
5. I recommend using flour that contains wheat that has been grown in Canada. This will help you make a strong, robust dough that will help reduce the chances of making the dreaded 'brick!' If you're in the UK or Europe then is the best bread flour to learn the fundamentals of bread making.
6. I recommend using a serrated tomato knife as this cuts fully-proved dough really well with less chance of either the dough gripping the knife as you cut, or causing collapsing of the dough.
7. Use a strong sandwich bag and cut a small hole 3–5 mm (¼ in maximum) in the bottom corner to use a piping bag as an alternative to purpose-made bags. Start with a very small hole and practice piping straight lines on the work surface (you can scrape this back into the back and re-pipe). You can always increase the size of the hole if it is too small.
8. If the bottom of your sweet pastry puffs up during baking, press it down with tissue (careful as it will release steam). Do this about 10 minutes into the bake as the pastry will still be flexible and not crack.
9. For large pastry tins it is best to leave the dough over hanging the top and press it against the side walls to help keep the pastry from falling inwards. Also, if you freeze, or at least chill the lined pastry tin before baking, it will hold its shape better. It will require a minute or two more baking especially if it was frozen when placed in your oven.

FACTS

FACT 1—Bulk fermentation
After the dough is fully kneaded, it is then left for a period of time called bulk fermentation. Generally this can be for 40–60 minutes.

I give my Sourdough two periods of bulk fermentation.

During the fermentation period the dough matures and naturally produces more gluten. A yeasted dough will also double in size. After which, it is gently degassed (knock back). This 'knock back', breaks down all the large gas bubbles into more uniform smaller bubbles which, when baked, will not only impart a finer crumb structure to the loaf, but also will make a stronger dough for the remainder of the process. Ultimately, less chance of the dreaded 'brick!'

FACT 2—Keeping Time
Sometimes just one timer might not be enough!

Agreed that this might seem a bit over the top but when you are baking you might potentially have four of five things on the go at any one time.

My advice is to write down next to each timer what task they are set for and you won't lose track of what you are doing.

HOW TO
Make your own proving box
This might appear simple, but believe me this works perfectly. All you need is a deep, lidded, plastic storage box. Place your tins or tray inside, put on the lid and leave to prove. If it needs a little warming up, place a cup with some boiling water inside. This will provide a little warmth and humidity inside the box. You can remove the cup if it gets too warm or wet.

Recreate oven bottom bread
Baking on the oven bottom in a bakery produces breads with exceptional crust. To recreate this in your own home oven you can use a pizza baking stone or a heavy metal upturned tray. Both must be preheated before placing the bread on top to bake. Gently place the fully-proved dough onto the baking stone using a pizza peel or a couple of fish slices.

Alternatively, if using an upturned tray, slide the dough onto the upturned tray, whilst it is still on the baking paper to prevent sticking to the tray.

Steam the oven

Creating steam in the oven at the onset of baking bread allows for the dough to fully expand before the setting of the crust, achieving maximum height to your bread. It also produces a crispier and shiny crust. To achieve this I recommend placing a roasting pan on the floor of the oven and allow it to get very hot. Place your dough into the oven then immediately pour some water into the roasting pan to create a generous amount of steam, then close the oven door to trap the steam. The dough rises and sets in the first few minutes of baking so don't delay in creating the steam.

CONTROLLING QUALITY

How do you know when your cake batter is light and fluffy?

In many cake recipes you might well be asked to mix the sugar and butter together until light and fluffy. That's a rather ambiguous statement which can naturally cause uncertainty.

When butter and sugar are mixed together they start to incorporate air, which makes the color of the batter turn pale (light) and the batter also become more voluminous (fluffy).

If these two ingredients are not thoroughly mixed there is a strong possibility that the batter will curdle when adding the egg, resulting in a reduction in height of the baked cake. To that end we need some kind of reference to ensure the batter has been thoroughly mixed before adding the egg.

So, behold the DIY paint color chart!

To utilise the paint color chart, firstly remove a small amount of batter after the butter and sugar are first combined. This is your initial batter reference. Place this reference against its closest color on the paint chart. Next, continue mixing until the batter looks 'white' compared to how it looked when just combined (you can take samples out before this stage to build up a step change in color as per illustration). When the batter looks 'white' in color, it has had enough mixing and is now ready to receive the egg.

TIPS AND TROUBLESHOOTING GUIDE FOR MACARONS

Italian or French method? The Italian method uses meringue which has boiled sugar added to it. I find this method produces a more robust macaron batter achieving more consistent results. The French method uses a classic meringue which has powdered sugar added. As the meringue in this method is softer, it can lose more air when combined with the ground almonds therefore producing a batter with too much flow.

Baking on two trays (one on top of the other) prevents the

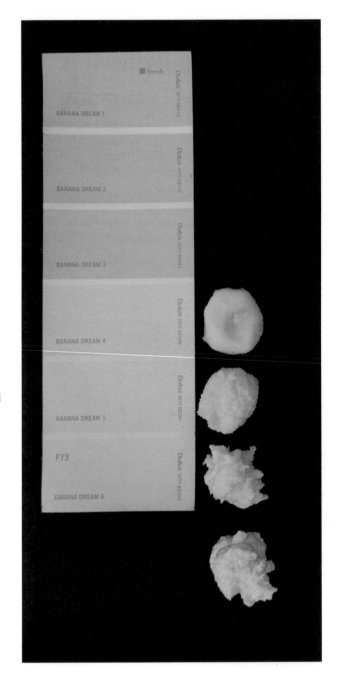

bottom of the shells baking too quickly, which would make it too hard and dry to eat. It also favours the formation of the famous feet (or crown), which is another macaron standard that can be frustratingly hard to get.

Aging egg whites means separating the whites from the yolks, and storing the whites in an airtight container in the fridge for 1 to two days before using them to make macarons. So why do you need to age egg whites? The reason behind it is to reduce the moisture content as much as possible while keeping the protein bonds from the egg whites the same. Also the aging process increases the whites' elasticity. If you skip this step, you might end up with a runny or watery batter, which will not yield great results. So age your egg whites, and take them out of the fridge, a few hours before making your macarons, to bring them up to room temperature before beating. eggs whisk better at room temperature.

Drying or resting the macaron shells before baking means to leave the piped discs, uncovered on the baking sheets, for 20 to 30 minutes, in a cool, dry place. This step will allow the batter to form a thin skin. The batter will lose its gloss and it should touch dry. Skipping this step will yield inconsistent results and cause all sorts of problems such as no feet or a warped shell.

The ideal batter consistency should form a thick ribbon that seems to flatten a bit when spooned but with a sturdy consistency. Many compare the right batter consistency to molten lava. Remember that it's always better to under beat than the contrary. A point to note is that as you transfer the batter to the piping bag, and then pipe the shells onto the baking sheets, the batter will continue to soften. If you overbeat before piping, you will end up with cracked or feetless macarons.

Tap the tray gently a few times before leaving to form a skin on the piped shells. This will release air bubbles trapped inside the piped shells. Eliminating this step can lead to strange cracks running diagonally on top, macarons split at the seams and o ozing into odd shapes, malformed feet in some places, footless in others.

Baking of macarons is tricky. Check your ovens temperature with a thermometer. Baking temperature should ideally be 150°C (300°F) to 160°C (325°F). It is best to bake macarons for a longer period of time so that the shells rise slowly but consistently. Fan ovens can be too fierce and potentially preventing the macarons from rising correctly.

No feet can be caused by the following:
- Batter is too thin.
- egg whites not aged.
- egg whites not beaten stiff enough.
- egg whites were left to stand for too long before incorporating into the almond/sugar/egg white mixture.
- The use of too much liquid food coloring.
- Batter was beaten too vigorously and too much air was knocked out of the meringue.
- Resting period is too short. The batter should have lost its shine and it should not stick to your finger before they are placed in the oven. If the weather is rainy or very humid, the resting period might take much longer.
- Resting period is too long—20 to 30 minutes resting period is usually enough.
- Oven temperature is too low (try raising your oven temperature by 10°C).

Uneven feet/feet bursting:
Oven temperature is too high. It's best to bake at a lower temperature 150°C (300°F) to 160°C (325°F) for a longer period of time so that the shells rise slowly but consistently.

Hollow shells:
- Piped shells have been resting for too long. 20 to 30 minutes resting period is usually enough.
- Oven temperature is too high, preventing the insides to set, causing the meringue to collapse when the shells are taken out of the oven. It is best to bake at a lower temperature 150°C (300°F) to 160°C (325°F) for a longer period of time so that the shells cook slowly but consistently.

Cracked shells:

- Oven temperature is too high. It is best to bake at a lower temperature 150°C (300°F) to 160°C (325°F) for a longer period of time so that the shells cook slowly but consistently.
- Resting period is too short. The batter should have lost its shine and it should not stick to your finger before the macaroons are placed in the oven. If the weather is rainy or very humid, the resting period might take much longer.
- Batter is too thin resulting in delicate shells.
- Batter was over mixed.
- Batter was under-mixed. If the batter is not mixed enough, too much air remains in the macarons, and the meringue dries out and cracks during the baking process.
- Too much moisture in the batter coming from underaged eggs or too much liquid coloring.
- Baking sheets not doubled.

Thin shells:

Over mixing results in a thin batter which will flow.

Warped and uneven shells:

- Batter is too thin.
- Too much moisture in the batter coming from under aged eggs or too much liquid coloring.
- Batter is over mixed.
- Oven temperature is too low. Try raising your oven temperature by 10°C and see if it helps.
- Resting period skipped or not long enough.

Shells seem too dry post bake:

Properly baked macaron shells always feel a little too dry at first. The magic happens when the macarons are filled, assembled and then left to mature for 24 hours. During this period moisture equilibrates between the center and the outside crust of the macaron, as well as the filling sandwiched between the two halves. This in turn softens the macaron into the delicate texture we have become accustomed too.

WEIGHING–GRAMS, OUNCES, CUPS AND SPOONS

To make consistently great products at home requires precision. Therefore I must stress that the importance of weighing your ingredients in grams is the most precise way. Weighing in ounces works, but becomes difficult when small amounts are required. There are 28.35 grams in every ounce, therefore if a recipe requires just 4 g of an ingredient, then that would be a little over one one-seventh of an ounce, which is not so easy to get precise! Generally, home baking recipes are small quantities and the smallest weight ingredients are most commonly the functional ingredients, yeast, baking powder and salt for example. If using teaspoons or ounces and you weighed the equivalent to 5 g instead of 4 g; that would be 25 per cent overweighed. That could significantly compromise your baked product. If you weighed in grams you would actually weigh 4 g precisely.

Using cups and spoons is extremely hit and miss, and will be the biggest cause of any home baking inconsistencies. Try this little test

at home. Fill your measuring cup level with flour (try to use the flour at the bottom of the bag as it is more compact). Tip this flour into a sieve and shake it through onto a sheet of paper. Now fill the same cup level with the sieved flour and see how much flour is remaining. This should highlight the variation you will get from using cups.

When weighing in grams you will have the same precise amount in your recipe every time, no matter how compact the ingredient is in the packaging.

It might seem daunting, swapping your longtime way of measurement from cups and spoons or ounces to grams, but it really is not that difficult. In fact it should make your measuring of ingredients a quicker process. A really accurate set of digital weighing scales are relatively inexpensive and will be a welcome addition to facilitate your precision baking at home.

All liquids should be weighed in grams too, and you will notice this is the case within the recipes found in this book. I highlight the inconsistencies of volumetric liquid measurement during my bread courses at Cinnamon Square when I weigh the water. Millilitres and grams are the same when it comes to water. Other liquids will differ, that is why oil floats on top of water because it is lighter. Therefore if I require 350 g of water for my bread dough, that will also equate to 350ml. I use a jug on the baking course which I place on the weighing scales and weigh 350 g of water. When the attendees look at the markings on the side of the jug it reads 400ml. Therefore, if we stop adding water when it reads 350ml on the jug we would only have about 300 g water. The resulting dough would be dry and tight, and if made into a loaf of bread, it would be the dreaded 'brick' again.

FREQUENTLY ASKED QUESTIONS
Static or convection oven?
I can guarantee someone will ask this question each time I teach a course at Cinnamon Square. My answer is always the same; a static oven is best for baking. When you consider what products we bake; bread, choux pastry, Danish pastry, cakes and sponges for examples, there is one thing they all have in common and that is that they are rising. Whether through fermentation from yeast, gas released from baking powder or steam trapped underneath the layers of fat, risers will all create rise within the product they are in. That rise takes place in the early part of the baking cycle. They will achieve their maximum potential rise if they are baked in a static oven. However, if the same products are placed in a convection oven they will face a continual blast of hot air which will form a crust sooner. Thus, restricting further gradual expansion and more than likely producing a slightly smaller product and quite often, unsightly breaking of the crust or sloping tops. I am not advocating you get a new oven, especially if you can't turn the fan off with your convection oven.

What's happening in the oven?
Have you ever wondered what is actually occurring within the doughs and batters when they go into the oven to bake?

Gases are formed like carbon dioxide and steam. Unless these gases are trapped, then they escape into the environment. Fortunately they become trapped by the proteins in the flour and the egg. The starches in flour gelatinise at 60°C (140°F) and this eventually forms the structure in many bakery products. The proteins in the flour and eggs coagulate from 74°C (165°F) and prevent further expansion. Therefore we require our products to reach maximum expansion before these dramatic changes occur. Moisture will evaporate from the product as it bakes. If you reweigh your baked product it can be 10–20 per cent lighter than when it entered the oven. The final major reaction is the formation of a crust and caramelization (browning), which contributes a lot to the flavor and texture. Once baked, the product cools and will continue to release moisture until it is wrapped.

TIP

If you spray the tops of the products with water before they are baked, it helps to slightly delay the crust from forming and subsequently achieve a better rise in the oven.

By machine or by hand?

In most of the recipes in this book I refer to mixing and kneading by hand. It is totally fine to use your mixer. In my courses at Cinnamon Square I try as much as possible to make everything by hand as I believe it is the best way to learn how and why each part of the process is important. You can feel and see the changes at a much closer level.

The main differences between the two methods is that a machine obviously makes life easier and it will mix to the optimum consistency, as long as you know what that consistency should be and then turn the machine off at that point. Therefore it is easy to over mix with a machine. Mixing by hand generally leads to under-mixing, and many attendees on my courses validate this point by commenting that, 'I never mix this long!'

White or wholemeal flour?

This can be a controversial subject. For me, I use whichever suits the product best. I personally prefer to eat white bread rather than wholemeal.

It is stated some of the nutrients in wholemeal flour pass through the body without being absorbed, unless used in long-fermented breads where more of the nutrients become available to the body. So for me, neither of them are really healthy or unhealthy, but I see them both as amongst of the most vital and functional ingredients in the bakers' store cupboard.

Why gluten is important?

The main source of gluten within baking comes from the protein contained in wheat flour. All wheat flour contains gluten. Bread flour contains the correct quantity and quality of gluten-forming protein to make bread, whereas plain (all purpose) flour will have less protein and of a different quality, and therefore will produce a weaker and less elastic dough. When bread making flour is hydrated and then manipulated during the kneading of the dough, the protein forms gluten; which is rather like creating a web of elastic bands within the dough. The newly-formed elasticity provides strength and shape to the dough, and it also withholds the gas produced by the yeast, subsequently allowing the dough to expand.

Intense stretching and folding of the dough during the kneading process will produce the maximum gluten from the flour, therefore producing a more forgiving dough for the remainder of the process, allowing the best possible loaf to be baked. Being too gentle will not bode well and there will be more chance in making the dreaded 'brick'. I always state on my courses, kneading is more of a workout rather than something therapeutic.

I like to use a simple garden trellis as an example to help visualise the role of gluten. The three pictures below illustrate the following:

Note: The trellis and elastic bands illustrate the gluten, and the ping pong ball represents a tiny bubble of the carbon dioxide gas produced from the yeast.

Picture 1. If the trellis is opened to the widest point, the ball can easily pass through the gaps. This highlights poor gluten development, which is unable to hold onto the gas.

Picture 2. If the trellis is closed a little then the ball cannot pass through. This now highlights the importance of gluten development and the newly-formed network of protein connections that can hold onto the gas, and will therefore allow for rising of the dough.

Picture 3. By connecting some elastic bands onto the trellis it now brings the trellis closer and tighter. This is highlighting further dough development; creating a stronger and more tolerant dough, attaining the most from the flour. This is the required dough consistency you will need to aim for when making most types of bread.

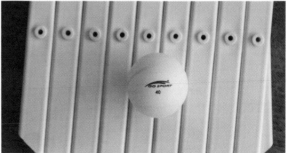

Salt in bread

Salt is an extremely functional ingredient in bread. It imparts flavor, controls yeast activity and strengthens the gluten. If you forget to add it to the dough, you will end up with a sticky mess. salt levels can be reduced slightly, but if reduced too much the dough ferments wildly, the structure will be weak and the resultant bread will be bland. In bread, salt is generally 1.8 per cent of the weight of the flour. It can be reduced to 1.5 per cent without significant detriment to the dough and baked bread.

It is possible to make bread without salt. The Tuscan bread in this book is salt-free. This is possible when making it by hand. It is much more difficult to make salt-free bread in large scale industrial baking because the processing equipment would not be able to cope with the significant changes to the doughs characteristics.

Fresh or dried yeast?

Most bakers use fresh yeast for their baking as it is cost effective. Fresh yeast must be kept refrigerated, and only has a short shelf life of 2–3 weeks. Dried yeast does not require refrigeration and it can last around 3 months. Dried yeast will actually be more consistent than fresh yeast. As a rule of thumb, dried yeast is used at half the level of fresh yeast.

There are two types of dried yeast. One requires soaking in water and sugar before use in order to get it activated. The other type is used just the same as fresh yeast, where it is added directly to the flour, salt and water. I recommend using the 'just add to flour' version. Within the recipes in this book I have given quantities for both fresh and dried variants.

You should see no major difference whether using fresh or dried yeast, and the flavor of the bread will not be compromised either. Most craft bakeries should let you have some fresh yeast. I give some to my customers free of charge. Make sure you ask your baker how old the yeast is when he gives it to you. This is important to know, as fresh yeast only has a short refrigerated shelf life and will gradually reduce its activity without you visually knowing.

Butter or margarine?

You won't find any margarine at Cinnamon Square as I only use butter in my recipes. I like to use authentic, traditional recipes containing traditional ingredients and therefore the use of butter is paramount for that. Yes, margarine whips up better and can be deemed more 'healthy' by some but butter's eating quality and the flavor it imparts is second to none.

If you prefer to use margarine in the recipes within this book then simply replace the butter by the same weight of margarine. Do not use the 'spreads' or 'low fat' varieties as they contain a lot more water and can be detrimental if used within some products. Also, the choice of margarine must be considered when making laminated pastry as it needs to be pliable to form and maintain layers when rolled.

Should dried fruit be soaked before use?

Although manufacturing hygiene is so much better today, you should at least wash dried fruit before using it to remove any potential dirt and debris. If you do this in hot water, it will soften the fruit slightly as it will absorb some water instantly.

When dried fruit is used within bakery products, the fruit will naturally take some of the moisture from the dough or batter. This results in drier baked products. After baking, the products will have a shorter edible shelf life as a consequence.

In breads and scones, where there is less water than in cakes, it is important to soak the fruit to retain the same eating qualities as there would have been if no dried fruit was added.

Soaking the dried fruit in alcohol is a great way of delivering intense flavor bursts inside a product they are used in. They can be left soaking for weeks to really mature. In my Stilton and Raisin Loaf recipe, the raisins could be pre-soaked in port, for example, complementing the cheese in the bread.

Silicone moulds or metal tins?

Silicone moulds can be used for baking bread and cakes. They can be purchased in many detailed shapes, are lightweight and very flexible. Home bakers find them useful, especially for the novelty shapes the moulds are made into, which can then be used to bake a fun child's birthday cake, for example. I see them targeted more as a home baker's product. You never see them in a craft bakery.

Personally I prefer to use metal pans and tins. The benefit of using metal tins is that the bake is so much better. As the tin heats up, it conducts this heat into the bread or cake inside. This facilitates the best possible bake, rise, crust and crust flavor.

Plain (all purpose) flour and high ratio cake flour?

Plain (all purpose) flour is a general purpose flour used for cakes, sponges and biscuits. It is milled from a soft wheat rather than hard wheat; which bread flour is made from. Cakes are made with higher levels of sugar

and liquids so in order to produce the modern softer and moister eating varieties, then a flour which absorbs more water is required, otherwise the products end up baked with a water-logged inside texture.

Years ago, plain (all purpose) flour was treated with chlorine to allow the flour hold on to more liquid. Today this process is banned in the UK, and an alternative heat-treated flour was developed. The gentle heat treatment slightly cooks the starch in the flour allowing it to absorb more water just as you do when cooking flour whilst making choux pastry. This flour is really good when making high liquid cakes like carrot or passion cake.

You won't find heat-treated flour in your local supermarket, but if you can get hold of some on the internet then I would recommend you buy some and try it. It is available to purchase in the Cinnamon Square shop, or on our website. Order it from us and we can post it out to you.

What is the best bread flour?

As with most things, the better the ingredients you put in, the better the product you get out. A premium quality bread making flour will produce a dough that will be more forgiving and tolerant throughout the entire bread making process. When you consider flour is two-thirds of the entire weight of a loaf of bread, we need to use one which is fit for purpose.

Bread making flour is produced from hard wheat. North America and Canada have the perfect climate to produce such flour. Here in the UK we produce good flour but when a premium bread making flour is required, it is commonplace to fortify UK grown wheat with some from North American and Canada. This flour is more expensive, but the resulting bread will be worthwhile. I use this type of flour at Cinnamon Square as standard, and it is possible for home bakers to purchase this in supermarkets too.

For novice home bakers, I recommend using such a flour while learning the fundamentals of bread making. Once confident in making bread at home, the new baker can try using locally grown and milled wheat flour, which will require a little more nurturing through the bread making process.

A 'Proper' bread tin?

Most bread tins you purchase in shops are generally too small to produce a decent loaf of bread. The main problem they all have is that the sides are too low. Although sold as a large bread tin, they are far from that. Have you ever made a loaf and it falls over the sides of the tin? This will be due to the incorrect tin size. What can also happen is that the user will place the bread tin in the oven too soon, due to the large amount of dough filling up the bread tin before it is actually fully proved.

Using my recipes and methods for the tin loaves in this book you will produce decent sized loaves. If the tin is not the correct size, you won't obtain the best loaf possible and end up with the inevitable overspill. You can purchase 'proper' bread tins on the internet and we sell them at Cinnamon Square too; in our shop or via our website.

The ideal size for a large bread tin is 23 cm (9 in) long, 12 cm (4¾) wide and 12 cm (4¾) deep. Aim to purchase something very close to this and you will make fantastic tin breads at home.

Tepid or cold water in a bread dough?
Many recipes will say to use tepid or cold water to make bread.

Never use cold water.

Yeast produces carbon dioxide gas in the dough, which in turn raises it. It will only do this if it is nice and warm. The colder the yeast becomes, the less active it will be. That is why you can place dough in the refrigerator overnight and it does not grow. Therefore, if you use cold water in your dough, the yeast will be less active, and if your recipe states to leave it to prove for one hour before baking; it will be under proved and too small to be baked. An experienced baker would then leave it longer before baking, but if you are following that recipe precisely, then you well have made the dreaded 'brick'.

You should always at least use tepid water, or if your room is cold then make it a little warmer. I aim to have my bread doughs at 25°C (77°F). This is an ideal temperature to make a nice calm, steady dough. If the dough is warmer I find it proves unnecessarily too fast, so remember; real bread takes time.

There is an actual formula to work out the correct water temperature to achieve my desired dough temperature:

Twice Desired Dough Temperature: (minus Flour Temperature = water Temperature)

Assuming I have tested my flour temperature and it read 20°C (68°F), the formula would be: 2 x 25 = 50–20 = 30°C (86°F)

Therefore to achieve a dough temperature of 25°C (77°F), I would need to warm the water to 30°C (86°F).

If you adopt the use of this formula to achieve the perfect water temperature, you will experience improved consistency of the breads made from it.

Kneading the dough on a bed of flour?
Never knead your dough on a bed of flour.

If you have a recipe that asks you to do that, unfortunately I would have to advise you to bin it! You won't find this procedure in any of my recipes in this book, nor in a craft bakery either.

If you consider that you would have meticulously weighed your ingredients to the nearest gram, mixed it in a bowl then placed it onto a bed of flour on the table, and you have now added who knows how many more grams of flour to the dough, you have now completely changed the initial recipe. The dough will now be drier and firmer than it should, and the resultant bread baked from it will be heavy and dense.

It is totally pointless and detrimental to knead dough on a bed of flour.

Even a very wet Ciabatta dough is not kneaded on a bed of flour; as then it would not be a wet dough anymore!

Flour is only used to process dough once it is fully kneaded. By that I mean when, by using a rolling pin, you pin out dough into shapes as for burger buns, or when cutting out ciabatta; it rests on a bed of flour to prevent it sticking to the table.

How to store and keep bread fresh?
The age old question 'how do I keep my crusty bread crusty?' All flour-based bakery products will stale and dry out and at varying rates. The more fat added to a product; the softer it initially is and the longer it will keep. Therefore a crusty loaf not containing any fat will not have a long shelf life. We are very aware of the French Baguette being purchased two and even three times a day, so it can be eaten at its best. That is because it stales and dries out so quickly. So how should this be stored if not eaten immediately? No matter how you store it, changes will still occur.

The best way to keep a baguette crusty is to place it in a paper bag. Unfortunately it will stale and dry in there, but it will keep true to how it should be eaten. If it is placed in a plastic bag instead it will stay moist inside but the crust will become chewy, and therefore the mouth feel will be completely different. The baguette could also sweat in the bag and grow mould.

So my answer to the original question is that bread is only fresh on the day it is made. Depending on the recipe, it will stale and dry out at different rates. So some breads are best eaten on the day they are made (baguettes and others will last a couple of days (tins and bloomers). Crusty breads are best kept wrapped in paper, and soft breads should be kept in plastic bags.

How to convert vanilla to chocolate?

Pastry, Cakes, Biscuits, Doughs can all be converted into chocolate versions by using unsweetened cocoa powder. The rule of thumb is to add 7 per cent cocoa based on the weight of flour, therefore 7 g (⅓ oz) cocoa powder per 100 g (3½ oz) flour. The trouble is that when you make one change for the better, there is generally a detrimental knock on effect. If the cocoa powder is added to the recipe, as well as adding chocolate characteristics, it will also make the product dry and tight. If you therefore remove flour of the same weight to allow for the added cocoa, it will make the product weaker and more fragile. This is when the skills of a product developer are useful, as they would consider options to compensate for the changes.

Adding melted real chocolate imparts even better chocolate flavors, but also brings fat and sugar to the recipe. Again, the recipe will require reconstruction to allow for the successful incorporation of real chocolate.

Knowing all of this, it probable makes sense to find a tried and tested chocolate recipe rather than create your own, unless you know a little about ingredient functionality and recipe balance.

FREEZING

I often get asked, by the attendees, at the end of my courses at Cinnamon Square whether the products they have just made can be frozen. Well, most bakery products can be frozen successfully. Items which might suffer from freezing include raw yeasted dough, fresh yeast, cream cheese (although when made into a frosting it is fine), whipped cream and chocolate.

My tips for freezing:
- Freeze the products as soon as possible after making them.
- Wrap the product tightly in strong food grade plastic bags and place them in plastic tubs.
- Never just place products loosely in a bag, as when you remove the bag from the freezer it might well contain ice. This ice will be the moisture which has migrated out of the frozen product. So when you then defrost this product it will be stale and dry.
- Place the freezing date on the packaging.
- Cut the product up before freezing to allow for portions to be removed individually.
- Cakes actually improve if frozen for a few days, especially if cutting shapes and decorating them for celebration cakes.
- Yeasted dough will freeze but the yeast activity will be compromised after defrosting and will prove much slower than if unfrozen, or not at all. Also the gluten structure is damaged from ice formation and weakens the dough. Bread made from this will be much smaller than the equivalent unfrozen dough.
- eggs can be frozen, but will lose some of their whipping properties compared to unfrozen.
- Cake batter can be frozen, but will lose a little baked volume compared to unfrozen. I would make sure the batter is frozen quickly to prevent any loss of raising agent activity. I would not recommend freezing sponge batter.
- Freezing unbaked pastry and biscuits is possible. Although, if butter is used in the recipe it will eventually go rancid, even though it is frozen. You can't tell by looking at it, but when it's defrosted you will note a 'cheesy' smell. I recommend discarding this. If you use this rancid pastry it will still smell and taste cheesy after baking.

Useful equipment required for your home baking

The pieces of equipment I have listed here are usedwithin this book and you will find them to be useful additions to your home baking tool kit.

Digital weighing scales
Timer
Digital thermometer
Lidded clear plastic boxes (various sizes
Plastic mixing bowls 25 cm (10 in) diameter
Large bread tin
Shower caps
Bowl scrapers
Baking paper
23 cm (9 in) round cake pan (loose-bottom)
23 cm (9 in) square baking pan
20 cm (8 in) round bundt cake pan
25 cm (10 in) round sponge pan—ideally with 5 cm (2 in) high sides
Serrated tomato knife
Hand spray bottle of water
Small pizza peel or a flat thin baking tray—for placing oven-bottom bread in oven
A meter ruler showing both millimetres and inches
Silpat (silicone pastry) baking mat
Blow torch
Crumpet rings
Florentine cases or bun cases

Useful ingredients required for your home baking

The ingredients I have listed might not be everyday items in your cupboard, but are used within my recipes in this book.

Ground rice or Semolina
Cream of tartar
Cake flour. This is a plain (all purpose) flour alternative which has been heat-treated to enable it to absorb more liquids and is therefore good for recipes like carrot cake.
Vegetable carbon powder
Medium polenta flour (Corn)
Glucose dyrup
Glycerine
Leaf gelatine
Mixed seed blends–sunflower, millet, flax, poppy, pumpkin, sesame for example.
White fat– cookeen, trex for examples.
Raw (demerara) sugar
Rye flour
Ground almonds
Fresh or dried yeast
bicarbonate of soda
Gluten-free plain and self-raising (self-rising) flour
Black treacle
Vegetable syrup
Jumbo oats (porridge)

INDEX

First published in 2016 by New Holland Publishers Pty Ltd
London • Sydney • Auckland

The Chandlery Unit 704 50 Westminster Bridge Road London SE1 7QY United Kingdom
1/66 Gibbes Street Chatswood NSW 2067 Australia
5/39 Woodside Ave Northcote, Auckland 0627 New Zealand

www.newhollandpublishers.com

Copyright © 2016 New Holland Publishers Pty Ltd
Copyright © 2016 in text: Paul Barker
Copyright © 2016 in images: New Holland Publishers Pty Ltd, Shutterstock

All rights reserved. No part of this publication may be reproduced, stored in a retrieval system
or transmitted, in any form or by any means, electronic, mechanical, photocopying, recording or
otherwise, without the prior written permission of the publishers and copyright holders.

A record of this book is held at the British Library and the National Library of Australia.

ISBN: 9781742578637

Managing Director: Fiona Schultz
Publisher: Diane Ward
Project Editor: Jessica McNamara
Designer: Lorena Susak
Photographer: Joanna Good
Production Director: James Mills-Hicks
Printer: Times Offset Malaysia

10 9 8 7 6 5 4 3 2 1

Keep up with New Holland Publishers on Facebook
www.facebook.com/NewHollandPublishers